Sleep Better Tonight

Unlock Meditation's Secrets to Overcome Insomnia

Experience the Healing Power of Meditation: A must-have guide for conquering sleep disorders.

By Evelyn Foster

Contents

Introduction

Welcome to a journey that will make nights, and by further extension, days change. Welcome to where meditation and sleep meet in their most profound depth. As you start flipping through these pages, you begin a journey to learn how to master sleeping peacefully with a very ancient yet ever-so-current practice: meditation. This is not just a handbook, but an extensively elaborated guide tailored for the needs of all those who, day after day, are lying on their bed, looking up at the ceiling, and trying to have the sleep that never shows up.

Sleep is a very active process in which the body and mind have to do a lot of work during this time that is absolutely necessary for health, cognition, and good mood. Yet, for many, sleep is a restless experience, punctuated by anxiety and a profound difficulty in transitioning from wakefulness to rest. This book is designed to address these challenges by unlocking the potential of meditation as a powerful tool for enhancing sleep quality.

You might wonder how a practice as seemingly simple as meditation can untangle the complex issues surrounding sleep. The following book tries to explain in detail the various ways meditation could calm a restless mind and invite restorative sleep to repair and rejuvenate the body. You will find various meditation techniques within these pages that scientific study has proven works in enhancing sleep patterns. These are not mere suppositions, but founded on sound research pointing to substantial sleep quality improvement, reduction in onset duration, and an increase in daily energy levels.

Furthermore, the practical advice given here is made to be accessible. Whether one is a new meditator or has an advanced practice, these strategies will be easily adopted into one's nightly routine. This will give step-by-step instructions on how to prepare for sleep through meditation, setting the stage for deeper and more consistent sleep cycles. You will learn focused attention practices, mindfulness meditation, body scanning, and more-skillful practices now empirically demonstrated to reduce bedtime anxiety and help create a sleep-conducive state of relaxation.

But this book goes beyond just techniques. It delves into the scientific underpinnings that explain why these practices are effective. You'll explore the neurological and physiological changes that occur during meditation—changes that mirror and enhance the natural processes our bodies undergo to prepare for sleep. This includes the reduction of cortisol levels, stabilization of the heart rate, and the cooling down of the brain's core, all of which are essential for initiating sound sleep. The goal here is not just to have a good night, but to develop a consistent and rewarding practice that will add to your general well-being. The benefits of meditation extend beyond the night: Regular practitioners report higher levels of overall happiness, lower stress throughout the day, and an increased capacity to navigate emotional storms. By incorporating meditation into your life, you are setting the foundation for better sleep and a more resilient state of mind.

In these pages, you will also find advice on creating the ideal environment that supports both meditation and sleep. From how to optimize your bedroom for tranquility, to understanding the impact of light and sound on your sleep cycle, this book covers all aspects of creating the perfect backdrop for rest. Since everyone's path to restful sleep can be as different as their fingerprint, you will learn how to make those practices and environments tailored to your needs.

This book is your companion in creating a nighttime routine that invites sleep and enriches your overall quality of life. You will notice coherence in the methods and motivations that interlink the practice of meditation with the science of sleep, with each chapter leading into the next. You will have a profound understanding of how meditation can enhance sleep by the end of this book, and the tools and confidence to apply this knowledge.

Embark on this journey with an open mind and a commitment to practice, and discover how the ancient art of meditation can be the key to unlocking the best sleep of your life. This is about overcoming not only insomnia but also embracing a lifestyle that cultivates vitality, peace, and well-being. Get ready to change your nights and reclaim your days.

The interaction between meditation and sleep is a very interestingly connected relationship that has widely been studied and debated in both scientific and wellness circles. At its core, the relationship hinges on the ability of meditation to modulate the body's stress response-a common culprit in sleep disturbances. The interaction necessary centers on how the methodology of meditation influences the autonomic nervous system through the mainly parasympathetic branch, as it has come to be described in everyday parlance as the "rest and digest" system. Breathwork, by its intrinsically rhythmic character-commonplace enough in many forms of meditation-interacts at the same level directly, introducing a response of relaxation that will of itself introduce sleep. In fact, by meditating, one can easily induce a downward spiral of physiological responses propitious for sleep: slowing of the heart rate, blood pressure reduction, and stress hormone level reduction. It's not just a question of becoming relaxed at the moment, but rather retraining the nervous system to reach this state with ease, which eventually will lead to more consistent sleep over time.

This relaxation effect is most useful for people suffering from insomnia, which is usually maintained by increased levels of arousal during periods leading up to bedtime. Most chronic insomniacs have an overactive sympathetic nervous system that could be toned down by regular meditation. By incorporating meditation into the nightly routine, one finds the transition from wakefulness to sleep less cumbersome. A more specifically, mindfulness meditation may help individuals develop a less reactive state when it is time to go to sleep, which has been evidenced to reduce sleep onset latency and increase sleep duration.

Besides, meditation supports deep stages of sleep, important for physical restoration and memory consolidation. It teaches the practitioner to shift the focus of attention away from anxieties of the day to a more introspective focus through techniques such as body scans and mindful awareness. This shift is not purely psychological; it has real physiological correlates. Brain imaging studies have proven that meditation increases the activity in brain regions responsible for attentional and emotive control, crucial to enter and maintain deep sleep states.

Consistent with this, neurochemical changes in the brain also reflect the relationship between meditation and sleep. Meditation has been associated with increased levels of melatonin, which is the hormone regulating sleep-wake cycles. By enhancing natural melatonin production, meditation helps align the body's internal clock, or circadian rhythm, which is often disrupted in individuals with sleep disorders. This alignment does not happen instantly, but rather develops through consistent, persistent practice. This hence shows the importance of having meditation incorporated as part of one's daily activities that will form part of the night routine.

Secondly, meditation helps in regulating emotional states for those in whose case anxiety, depression, or stress disrupts their sleep. The practice creates an emotionally balanced state and lessens the occurrence of mental states that cause sleep disruption. It's about creating a buffer between the mind and those racing thoughts and worries that strike in the night. It would then be regarded not only as a prophylactic against sleep disturbances through emotional distress but also therapeutic.

Meditating for good sleep therefore tends to foster an overall life behavior of attitudinal change toward oneself through being mindful and caring; these will have fringe effects on sleeping. As already pointed out, a regular practitioner of meditation is most likely to embrace other habits known to positively influence the occurrence of a good quality and quantity of sleep-wake cycle.

As useful as these practices are, the trick to making them work most effectively is consistency and devotion. The effects of meditation accumulate over time, as improvements in both quality and length of sleep tend to improve gradually as a person develops their skills at meditating. Hence, encouragement to persist with the practice is important. One must be patient while approaching meditation and also acknowledge that the benefits accrue and tend to become apparent much later as one keeps on practicing it for sleep.

This involves persisting in meditation regularly, whether it is perceived as difficult or the improvement in sleep is not as rapid as one would like. Gradually, the mind and body learn to move into states of relaxation more easily, and meditation and sleep deepen. In a nutshell, meditation trains the practitioner to take gentle yet firm control of his or her physiological and psychological processes to facilitate sleep, proving quite a powerful, accessible, and sustainable tool in the pursuit of better health and well-being.

Improvement in sleeping through meditation can be likened unto the cultivation of a garden: just as with a garden, improvement with meditation is gradual and requires time and regular attention. Cultivating good habits takes care and persistence since the fruits of one's labor often do not show up overnight. This being the case, anyone looking to investigate the healing dimensions of meditation with a view to conquering sleep disorders needs to recognize that improvements in sleep usually come progressively-perhaps subtly at times.

This tendency to get quick results might be a natural human instinct, and one may just quit meditation if sleep does not improve dramatically right away. However, the benefits of meditation in enhancing sleep are cumulative over time and with consistency. Commitment to regular meditation is more than a routine; it's a commitment to a lifestyle change, a decision to invest in one's long-term health and well-being.

Setting realistic expectations is one of the most pivotal elements in building a consistent meditation practice. It is good to understand that progress in meditation and its impact on sleep is gradual. Some nights will be better than others, and that is normal. This is part of the learning and adapting your body and mind will go through. Understanding and accepting fluctuations in the quality of sleep can reinforce perseverance and reduce frustration.

Encouraging a regular meditation schedule helps to develop, in a manner of speaking, a new muscle-a skill that is nurtured through practice. Much as athletes train regularly to optimize performance, so too must people who wish to improve their sleep through meditation practice regularly for the best possible results. Such consistency in practice embeds the relaxation response in the nervous system and makes the process more natural during sleep.

Besides, a good environment for practice may also play a very critical role in consistency. Designate a specific time and place to meditate-preferably quiet and without interruption. This could be a corner of a room set up with a comfortable seat or cushion, perhaps with some elements that induce calm, such as soft lighting, a scented candle, or calming sounds. A specific place, on the other hand, will enhance the quality of the practice itself but also reinforce the habit through associating that space with mindfulness and relaxation.

Meditation could be incorporated into the pre-sleep phase to help bridge that particular gap between wakefulness and sleep. It would tell the body and mind through this activity that it's time to slow down toward rest. This could be just a few minutes of breathing or a full session, from guided imagery to body scan techniques, depending on preference and personal fit.

It is also good to keep a meditation and sleep journal. This will be quite helpful in showing patterns and progress, and, therefore, could provide insight as to what works and what does not. Noticing a trend over time can prove to be quite motivating, informative, and helpful while adjusting practices to better fit individual needs for sleep.

The process may be further encouraged by participating in a community of individuals who are trying to sleep better with meditation. Whether this is through an online forum, a local meditation group, or even a course, knowing other people in the same shoes will make the reinforcement much easier on commitment and have many tips and emotional support.

It is good, when feeling demotivated, to reflect on the benefits that have already been accrued and remind oneself why it was started in the first place-to improve sleep through meditation. Whether this is about feeling more rested, having more energy during the day, or simply enjoying the quietness of the mind, these personal victories tend to be very powerful motivators in continuing.

Lastly, be open to investigating and adapting various meditation practices. There are a wide range of practices in mindfulness and meditation that suit many different personalities and needs. While some find peace in the stillness of meditation, others might connect more with movement-based practices like yoga or tai chi. This flexibility not only keeps the practice interesting but also amplifies the ability to deal with sleep disruptions when they do occur.

Better sleep is not only a question of persistence in meditation practices, but the development of awareness that permeates every instance in life for greater emotional balance and physical health. The deep commitment to the recapture of night-that is, transformation of those hours of possible turmoil into a haven peacefully replenishing both mind and body. By committing to this path with patience and regularity, the journey itself becomes as rewarding as the destination.

Understanding Sleep and Insomnia

Sleep, a vital, involuntary process, is as crucial to our bodies as water or food. Understanding its complexities can transform our approach to rest, particularly when addressing issues like insomnia. This exploration begins with delving into the stages and cycles of sleep, components that are foundational to recognizing why our nights may be restful or restless.

We sleep in cycles of about 90 to 120 minutes, within which our brains go through several distinct stages. These have been categorized into NREM sleep, further divided into three phases, and REM sleep, each serving a different function critical to brain health and general well-being.

The first stage of NREM is the lightest. It is the time when your brain begins to shut itself off from the sensations of the outside world, a time ranging between 1 and 7 minutes. It is when one is in a mild wakefulness and can readily be disturbed. This phase acts like the entrance to deeper sleep, with the body slowing down and the heartbeat and breathing becoming slower.

The second stage of non-REM sleep is a deeper sleep stage. About 45-55% of total sleep in adults is composed of this stage. During the process, one's body becomes relaxed: heart rate continues to decline and the body temperature drops. Importantly, this stage features bursts of brain activity known as sleep spindles and K-complexes, which are believed to protect the brain from awakening from sleep and also play a role in consolidating memories and learning. Most of our nightly rest occurs during this stage of sleep.

The third and final stage of NREM is usually referred to as deep sleep or slow-wave sleep, and is essential for physical recovery and growth. It is during this phase that the body repairs muscles and tissues, stimulates growth and development, boosts immune function, and builds up energy for the next day. This stage is characterized by delta waves, which are the slowest and highest amplitude brain waves, reflecting the deepest levels of relaxation and disengagement from the external environment. This is followed by REM sleep at the peak of the cycle, a stage characterized by rapid movements of the eyes. During REM, or rapid eye movement, sleep, the brain behaves like it does when awake-the paradoxical stage of sleep. It is also emotionally important for emotional processing and memory consolidation, allowing for creativity. During REM, the body has atonia, which refers to a temporary paralysis in the muscle groups to keep one from acting out one's dreams. This is an important stage for cognitive functions: problem-solving and memory consolidation.

When one cycle is complete, the sleep cycle begins again, briefly returning to the lightest stage of NREM before moving into the deeper stages and back into REM. Across the night, the length of each cycle may change; the earlier cycles include longer periods of deep sleep, while the later cycles tend to be lighter and include more REM sleep.

This cyclic pattern of stages during sleep is important in understanding how and why disruption to these cycles leads to disorders such as insomnia. Disturbances in the rhythm and timing of these stages—due to stress, environmental factors, or health problems—greatly influence the restorative quality of sleep. Individuals with insomnia may wake up numerous times during the night, or they may spend an inordinate amount of time in light sleep; either condition can produce daytime fatigue and a constellation of other symptoms. Mastery of these cycles provides the background necessary to understand the common causes and symptoms of insomnia, many of which involve direct interference with the normal progression through the stages of sleep. By understanding the basic sleep science, we set the stage for more focused and effective interventions in targeting specific disruptions in the individual sleep architecture. This not only illustrates the pathways through which sleep disorders manifest, but also expands our capacity to devise interventions that restore the natural balance of sleep stages towards optimum health and well-being.

The complex nature of insomnia can be explored in the various factors that can trigger this common sleep disorder. It is not a symptom, but a complex condition influenced by psychological and physiological aspects that can disrupt anybody's life.

Stress is one of the important provocations toward insomnia. At any point, life demands from job and family expectations to the shocks of unexpected setbacks like the sickness or loss of one's resources all seem to catch a toll regarding going to or remaining in sleep. The mental stresses switch on the sympathetic nervous system by quickening heart rates, blood pressures, increasing tenseness in the muscles, or heightening alertness-a very prop to wakefulness, rather than rest or sleep.

Apart from stress, the other psychological factors are anxiety and depression. These conditions can be related to sleep disturbances in the way that anxiety may interfere with the induction of sleep, while depression often causes early morning awakenings or hypersomnia, a condition wherein one sleeps a great deal but never feels rested. Anxiety activates the arousal system of the body, which inhibits the ability to relax, while depression impacts neurotransmitters related to sleep regulation and interferes with the normal sleep cycle.

Behavioral factors also bear significance in sleep health. Poor sleep hygiene, which can be going to bed at odd hours, performing exciting activities before bedtime, or inappropriate sleep environment, all help cause insomnia. A simple example would be that the light emitted from computers and electronic reading devices can suppress melatonin production, the hormone that lets our bodies know it's time to go to bed. In the same vein, caffeine consumption later in the day-which is the habit of many-is an enemy of sleep because it can prolong the time required to fall asleep.

Medical conditions can also physiologically set off insomnia. Such examples include chronic pain, asthma, allergies, neurological disorders, and hormonal imbalances. Sleep disturbances are caused in any of these instances. For example, individuals who are suffering from chronic pain do not find a sleeping posture that is comfortable, and on certain occasions, they awake from sleep due to this pain. Similarly, in respiratory conditions, patients may wake up due to shortage of breath.

This will similarly attribute to insomnia: medications for different conditions. Some antidepressants, heart and blood pressure medications, allergy medications, and stimulants can interfere with sleep. People who take this type of medication should start consulting their health providers about potential side effects on sleep and possible alternatives or adjustments in their treatment regimens that could mitigate such impacts.

Our sleep-wake cycle is regulated by the circadian rhythm, or our body's internal clock, which may be disrupted due to various causes contributing to insomnia. Jet lag, resulting from traveling through time zones, night shifts at work, or artificial light during nighttime, may interfere with this internal clock. An improper alignment of the circadian rhythm contributes to insomnia in the form of extreme difficulties with sleeping at desired times and waking up on time.

Lifestyle and environmental factors are also playing a great role in sleep. The sedentary life reduces the quality of sleep. Regular physical activity is important for getting more restful and deeper sleep. Overstimulation in the sleeping environment, like noisy bedrooms or very hot beds, interferes with good sleep for sure. Thus, creation of a restful environment and maintenance of a lifestyle promoting good sleep is an essential step in insomnia management.

The symptoms of insomnia are very broad, ranging from poor initiation of sleep, poor maintenance of sleep, or early morning waking when one cannot get back to sleep. Major daytime symptoms include fatigue, mood disturbances, reduced efficiency in work, and a general sense of not feeling well both psychologically and physically. Cumulatively, sleep deprivation leads to not only fatigue but also further advanced health complications like poor immune response, pain sensitivity, hypertension, and eventually higher vulnerability to chronic diseases over a period of time.

Recognizing these causes and symptoms helps the professionals address the far-reaching ramification of sleep loss on health and wellness. Poor sleep affects nearly every facet of our lives: psychological, physical health, and, overall, the quality of life. In consideration of the roots and manifestations of insomnia, there will be opportunity for patients and providers to make more thorough and effective strategies for managing sleep disturbance and improving nighttime rest and daytime vitality. This is not only proactive for immediate insomnia, but also promotes long-term health and wellbeing, a way of demonstrating how sleep fits within the overall paradigm of health.

The results of sleep deprivation reach far beyond the fatigue factor into nearly all aspects of a person's health and everyday functioning.

Sleep is like diet and exercise in that it is a basic component of health. It is crucial for brain function, physical health, and quality of life.

From an immediate, devastating toll on multiple systems of the body to contributing to the development of chronic conditions, sleep deprivation can have immediate and devastating effects. The first casualty when sleep eludes us is our brain. Without enough rest, cognitive abilities, including memory, decision-making, and reasoning skills, deteriorate.

While the brain is asleep, mainly during deep REM stages, it processes and consolidates memories from the day. Without these crucial phases of sleep, short-term memories struggle to transfer into long-term storage, making learning more challenging.

Furthermore, creativity and solving problems dwindle because the brain relies a lot on downtime to knit together new ideas and solutions from daily experiences. Emotionally too, sleep deprivation exacts a similarly strict toll: the overreaction of the amygdala when one does not get enough sleep thus leads to irritability heightened by stress while the prefrontal cortex responsible for judgment and control of impulses becomes less active. This can increase mood swings and worsen symptoms of anxiety and depression, among other mental health disorders. Thus, it is no surprise that sleep is usually the first treatment that mental health professionals recommend improving.

From a physiological perspective, the effect is wide-ranging and varied. Sleep modulates many bodily activities, including the exocrine secretion of hormones throughout the body, from maintaining energy to appetite. Poor sleep interferes with the production of several key hormones regulated by the endocrine system, including insulin, an essential regulator of blood sugar. With this, sleep deprivation is strongly linked to an increased risk of type 2 diabetes due to reduced effectiveness in the body's use of insulin.

Further, insufficient rest impairs cardiovascular health. Blood pressure and heart rate are higher when sleep is poor. The body needs rest to preserve endothelial function and the vascular smooth muscle tone, both of which are essential to cardiovascular health. Chronic sleep deprivation over time leads to severe heart conditions, such as hypertension, and a high risk of stroke and heart attack.

Sleep is also a major player in immune function. While sleeping, the body produces cytokines, which are proteins that help the immune system in its battle against infections and inflammation. When a person does not get enough sleep, cytokine production is reduced, and the immune cells of the body do not attack invaders as aggressively. This suppression can lead to heightened vulnerability to viruses and prolonged recovery periods from illness.

Chronic sleep deprivation has also been associated with longer-term metabolic issues, including obesity and the deregulation of appetite-controlling hormones ghrelin and leptin. Ghrelin signals the brain about feelings of hunger, while leptin conveys satiety. The body, when starved of sleep, manufactures more ghrelin and less leptin, thus creating the feeling of hunger and a higher consumption of calories.

These effects spill over in the way one looks too: a lack of sleep can result in the skin aging prematurely and increased signs of aging. Sleep reduces the resiliency of skin to environmental elements such as sunlight. It is during deep sleep that our bodies are repairing themselves from the rigors of the day, something without which a person would feel slower to heal or recover from wounds.

Apart from the obvious health consequences, sleep deprivation significantly affects everyday life. Work performance is less efficient, with a decrease in concentration and higher incidence of work accidents. Activities where one needs to be highly alert and take quick measures are also risky, such as driving a car. In fact, driving because of sleepiness causes thousands of traffic accidents and deaths every year.

With such wide-reaching and deep impacts, it becomes critical that sleep be a priority and interventions sought where necessary. The possible long-term health complications arising from continued sleep deprivation make it important to take proactive steps in improving the quality and quantity of sleep. It is a vital area of health, one that should be placed right up there with nutrition and exercise, as it is fundamentally associated with the optimal function of nearly all systems in the body.

Knowing the serious outcomes of sleep deprivation, one can understand effortlessly why quality sleep is not an option but a must for anyone desiring to live a healthy and vibrant life. The path to better sleep may require changes in lifestyle, environment, and even medical intervention, but the payoff in well-being and longevity makes such efforts priceless.

The Basics of Meditation

While most people imagine meditation as a monk in complete silence on top of a mountain, it can be much more accessible and varied than most people initially consider. This ancient art, which has threaded its way through countless cultures and epochs with threads of tradition, offers deep benefits that are innately part of the mind's natural capacities. It essentially involves the development of a special state of awareness combined with focused attention-a concept so amazingly simple and deeply transformative at the same time.

Meditation, in its very essence, is a training in attention to develop mental clarity and emotional calm by focusing attention on an object, a thought, or an activity. Contrary to common conceptions of meditation, it does not change personality, introduce a new personality, or empty the mind. Rather, it is to learn not to judge anything but observe, to give space to understand one's thoughts and feelings without being clogged by them.

The notion that the right way to meditate is to make the mind free of thoughts is a mistaken belief. What this practice does is train attention so that there may be better, more voluntary control over what the mind focuses on. When the mind wanders during meditation-as it will-the practice is simply to notice it has wandered and gently bring focus back to whatever object of attention one has chosen.

Another common myth is that meditation is some sort of religious practice. While it is true that meditation forms an integral part of many religious and spiritual traditions, the practice per se stands independent of any religious line and can thus be availed of as a secular tool aimed at enhancing mental health and general well-being. It is a method, so to say, dealing with the mind and its functions, serving all people irrespective of any religious or spiritual background.

Another myth about meditation is that it is usually presented as something only those with ample time can practice, but there is nothing further from reality. Meditation can be quite organically incorporated into daily routines through the use of a couple of minutes each day. It does not have to include hours of motionless silence but can be taken in small blocks that fit literally into all schedules and lifestyles. Be it a few minutes of mindful breathing every morning or a brief meditation on the lunch break, flexibility is what allows this skill to be an option for literally anyone.

The benefits of meditation, when done regularly, are robust and wide-ranging: from reducing stress and controlling anxiety to promoting emotional health and enhancing self-awareness. It can also improve attention, probably increase memory, and extend cognitive sharpness. Physically, it can help reduce age-related memory loss, help with fighting addictions, improving sleep, helping in pain control, and decreasing blood pressure.

The effectiveness of meditation is derived from increasing awareness of the present moment. By focusing on the now, many practitioners of meditation often gain a greater appreciation of the moment and also become less preoccupied by anxieties of the past or concerns about the future. In this sense, such present-centeredness can result in greater peace in daily life and improved resistance to the impact of various stressors.

It also fosters more profound empathy and connection with other people. Meditation can help develop better interpersonal relationships and improve communication by increasing the ability to attune to one's feelings and those of others. This emotional connection arises from heightened awareness and acceptance of one's thoughts and feelings cultivated through regular practice.

Other misunderstandings about meditation may be due to its depiction in popular media as a quick fix or even a magic solution to life's challenges. Meditation indeed has many benefits, but it needs practice regularly and is most effective within a routine. Like any skill, the benefits of meditation develop over time and with practice. It is not something that cures everything, yet it is a tool-one that allows the focusing of attention to bring balance and equanimity to the mind and body. Meditation is a practice that goes down to deep and profound levels, offering an unprecedented opportunity for life improvement. Standing as a testament to the immense capabilities of the human mind stands the fact that its function and well-being can be influenced so easily by acts of attentiveness. The following diversity of meditation types will even more strongly suggest the versatility and adaptability of this practice in pointing clearly to the path toward peace, resilience, and mindful presence in everyday living.

The diverse landscape of meditation offers many practices each designed to enhance mental and physical well-being through various techniques of attention and focus; in such diversity, one often finds a form which suits one's preference and needs, contributing a great deal to stress reduction, relaxation, and psychological growth.

Focused attention meditation is a foundational style that places the practitioner's attention onto one object, thought, or sound. This can be as basic as focusing on your breathing, the flame of a candle, or some simple mantra repeated silently. This practice includes bringing the mind back to its focus whenever it wanders. This trains the mind to increase its ability to maintain focus and attention, which are significant features for personal and professional effectiveness.

Another popular form of meditation is mindfulness meditation, which builds a great awareness of the present moment. During this form of meditation, one does not focus on one point but rather observes everything in the environment, such as thoughts, sounds, sensations in the body, or whatever happens around them. Mindfulness aims at developing heightened awareness to increase one's response to stress, understanding personal habits, and emotional responses to difficult situations. Another major type is transcendental meditation, which uses the mantra-one that is given out loud in silence, in a specific manner. This style of meditation is known for deep relaxation, release of stress; therefore, it is often taught by a certified instructor who can provide a personal mantra to utilize in daily sessions. The repetition of the mantra serves to transcend the practitioner from the present state of active mind to a state of pure consciousness, hence increasing overall mental clarity and restfulness.

Loving-kindness meditation, also known as Metta meditation, practiced cultivating a feeling toward everything, even sources of stress and one's enemies of loving and compassion. For themselves, the practitioner begins cultivating an attitude of acceptance of themselves, and allows one of kindness and love towards themselves, extending this goodness further out in a circle from friends, acquaintances and all beings. Anxiety decreases and social connectedness improves; thus, this type of meditation should be a useful intervention for patients displaying social anxiety or feelings of hostility.

The technique in the method of body scan or progressive relaxation is such that a person's attention is brought onto the different parts of his or her body. These two practices help one notice various sensations of tension and warmth. These exercises generate an awareness of body sensation and integration of the mind with the body, thus leading to increased ability to relax both the mind and body.

Moving meditation-Tai Chi, Qigong, and some forms of yoga-develop concentration, flexibility, and physical strength by combining meditation with fluid movements. The gentle, flowing movements are deeply focused and performed in a very attentive way to balance energy in the body, maintaining health and well-being.

Visualization, or guided imagery, is a very relaxing type of meditation in which you can visualize a scene in which you are at peace, free to let go of all tension and anxiety. This usually takes the form of meditation led by either a recording or a teacher; therefore, it is great for beginners and also helpful for those for whom relaxation may be difficult to achieve.

Each of these will have various advantages and different positive influences on the brain and body. For instance, it has been documented that meditation with focused attention improves one's ability to concentrate and extend the span of attention. Mindfulness is good at reducing ruminations of negative feelings, emotional flexibility, and improving one's ability to engage in new or challenging situations without being overwhelmed.

With the mind getting used to being in that meditative state through any of these practices, it would be able to handle stressors better and keep a peaceful mental environment even outside meditation sessions. Such a transition of skills is significant for long-term benefits, since regular practice embeds these capabilities deeper into daily life.

These various forms of meditation allow one to choose the kind of practice or combination that best fits one's lifestyle and psychological needs. Thus, one will be in a better position to practice regularly when it comes to personal meditation, enjoying profound benefits accruing from meditation: reduced stress and anxiety, improved focus, greater emotional resilience, and so on. While further detailing how such practices impact both the brain and the body, one starts to get the feeling that meditation cannot be characterized merely as an escape from pressures, for it is also a profoundly transformative tool fostering health and well-being long afterward.

The influence of meditation on the brain and body has been immense, with many scientific studies focusing on how this ancient practice enhances both mental and physical health. The following exploration goes deep into the ways in which meditation changes neural pathways and physiological processes to lay a foundation for improved health and increased vitality.

Meditation not only changes the brain structurally but also in the way it functions, hence causing observable changes in brain scans: increased thickness in those areas of the brain presiding over attention, introspection, and sensory processing. Consistent meditation practice causes the prefrontal cortex, important in higher order brain functions like awareness, concentration, and decision-making, to become more active and densely packed with neurons. This improvement in the prefrontal cortex underlies a parallel enhancement in improved cognitive abilities and better handling of stress, allowing one to be resilient after any adverse situation.

Meditation enhances neuroplasticity, or the powers of self-reorganization by forming new neural connections within the brain. The brain becomes more capable of adapting to new experiences and learning and remembering them. During meditation, this relaxed state encourages the production of neurotransmitters that induce well-being, such as serotonin, dopamine, and endorphins. These changes contribute to improved mood and behavior.

Besides that, the amygdala is also known as the "fight or flight" center in the brain. It will be less active, and meditation has lower gray matter density during a routine meditation practice; these facts correlate with reduced anxiety and stressful reactions. The feeling of serenity and composure, which indicates meditation, results from how the brain is informed not to respond in a harsh or startled way even when dreadful or surprising situations arise.

On a physiological level, meditation works its magic by modulating the autonomic nervous system that regulates unconscious bodily functions such as heartbeat, digestion, and respiratory rate. It increases the activity of the parasympathetic nervous system associated with relaxation and rejuvenation, while reducing activity in the sympathetic nervous system linked to the stimulation of the body's stress response. The end result is that regular meditators will usually have reduced blood pressure, better blood circulation, and a reduced heart rate, thereby contributing to healthy cardiovascular functioning.

The effect on the endocrine system is also significant because meditation tends to normalize hormone levels. By reducing the level of cortisol and adrenaline released as a result of stress, meditation can prevent some adverse effects of chronic stress, which are suppressed immune function and the increased risk for many chronic diseases, including hypertension, cardiovascular disease, diabetes, and specific cancers.

Meditation has also been shown to boost the immune system by increasing the body's antibody response. This could imply that meditators are less likely to get sick, and when they do get sick, they recover much faster from all sorts of health issues. The relaxation response produced by meditation releases nitric oxide into the blood, causing blood vessels to dilate and blood pressure to decrease. This biochemical change not only improves cardiovascular health but also plays a role in increasing sexual arousal, which is often suppressed by stress and anxiety.

The gastrointestinal system, which is sensitive to stress and emotion, benefits from the calming effects of meditation. Improved digestion and alleviation of gastrointestinal symptoms are often reported by those who engage in regular meditative practices. This is likely due to enhanced parasympathetic activity, leading to more efficient digestion and absorption of nutrients.

Meditation also affects such complex conditions as chronic pain, influenced by both psychological and physiological factors. It was proven that meditative practices may change pain perception, decrease the severity of chronic pain, engage those brain regions which take part in pain regulation, and reduce anxiety and depression that usually accompany chronic pain conditions.

Sleep, one of the most important yet forgotten aspects of overall health, is greatly impacted by meditation. Meditation serves to quicken the time it takes to fall asleep and increases deep sleep by helping one to relax and work out active cognitive processes that prevent sleep, such as a racing mind or anxiety. This ensures not only better sleep quality but also gives the body greater efficiency in the repair and regeneration processes it undergoes during sleep.

In summary, pervasive mediation between brain and body, again, demonstrates that meditation is generally holistic in nature. From an ancient practice, which offered solutions to many of our present-day health challenges at inexpensive costs and easy accessibility, there isn't much that can be seen for individual benefits or contribution toward living and sharing a healthy, wise, and peaceful society.

The Scientifically Proven Benefits of Meditation for Insomnia

Insomnia is a prevalent condition affecting millions of people in the world, thus creating a pressing need for efficient and effective long-term interventions. The complexity of insomnia includes a range of symptoms such as difficulties initiating sleep, maintaining sleep, or experiencing non-restorative sleep that notably impairs a person's daily functioning. Traditionally, the management of such symptoms has relied heavily on pharmacological treatments, which, though effective in the short run, result in long-term dependencies and a host of undesirable side effects ranging from gastrointestinal distress to cognitive impairments. In this regard, there is an increasing call for support of alternative non-pharmacological therapies that will alleviate symptoms but also target the root causes of insomnia.

Meditation, being the practice deeply rooted in the betterment of mental and physical balance, therefore presents itself as a very befitting, evidence-based solution in this context. The practice of meditation-particularly mindfulness and guided relaxation-has shown great promise in clinical settings, helping individuals cultivate a state of calm, focused relaxation that can significantly enhance the onset and quality of sleep. In meditation, a person trains in regulating one's response to stress, which would lead to less anxiety and induce a natural sleep onset-all factors usually disrupted in a person who suffers from insomnia.

Meditation to improve sleep is not anecdotal; it has behind it a growing body of scientific evidence that underlines its benefits, hence making it an essential component of sleep hygiene practices that are prescribed by health practitioners. Many studies have described how meditation changes the autonomic nervous system, reduces hyperarousal, and resets sleep patterns, thereby greatly improving sleep quality with no side effects associated with the use of sleeping medications.

Besides benefits related to sleep, meditation contributes to general health, improving emotional regulation and resilience, increasing pain tolerance, and strengthening the immune system-all of which are in bad need among those suffering from chronic insomnia. Meditation has been associated with increased levels of melatonin, the sleep On/Off hormone, and changes in brain activity toward those that favor sleep. Meditation turns on parts of the brain associated with deeper stages of sleep, thus making sleep both more available and more restorative.

Moreover, meditation practices raise one's awareness of thoughts and feelings and allow a person to detach from these vicious circles of stress and anxiety that contribute so much to sleep disturbances. The person will be able to have a more mindful attitude toward sleep and pre-sleep behavior, which would drastically shorten the time it takes to fall asleep and prolong the deep sleep period.

This emphasis on evidence-based approaches in treating insomnia underscores the commitment not only to the understanding of root causes that may be causing sleep disturbances but also to long-term, sustainable, and health-promoting interventions. Meditation, being a non-invasive and accessible therapeutic tool, fits all these goals of promoting sleep improvements that are scientifically and experientially validated. As we delve into the specific studies and research that validate meditation's role in improving sleep quality, it becomes clear that integrating meditation into daily routines is more than a wellness trend; it is a basic building block of a healthy lifestyle that can transform our nights and, by extension, our days. By accepting the regular practice of meditation, this can be the catalyst that changes our experience with sleep from frustrating-elusive to rest-rejuvenation and in the process optimizes all dimensions of health. Not only would individual health improve with a change in sleep behavior, but possibly public health through reduced dependency on medication and cultivating an empowered, self-sufficient approach to health maintenance.

The empirical evidence that meditation is effective in enhancing sleep quality is strong, based on many controlled trials and research studies that elaborate on the beneficial impacts on both mind and body. Much interest has been shown by the scientific community in unearthing how meditation contributes to improved sleep quality, thus providing a wealth of data that affirms its therapeutic benefits.

Among the main researches, one of the most noticeable works is the study of Stanford University, which explored the effects of mindfulness meditation on a group of people suffering from insomnia. The subjects engaged in mindfulness to develop an awareness of their present surroundings and their current state for six weeks. Results indicated not only a significant reduction in time taken to fall asleep but also improvements in total sleep time and quality. This well-set study laid the ground for further exploration into how directed mindfulness exercises could ameliorate symptoms of insomnia. Equally, a randomized clinical trial published in the journal JAMA Internal Medicine took a look at 49 middle-aged and older adults who reported trouble sleeping. Half of the participants were given a mindfulness awareness program that taught meditation and other exercises to help them pay attention to moment-by-moment experiences, thoughts, and emotions. The remaining participants took a sleep education class that taught ways to improve sleep habits. At the end of the study, the mindfulness group had less insomnia, fatigue, and depression than the sleep education group.

Another powerful body of research involves a meta-analysis of over 18 studies, with over 1,150 total participants suffering from sleep disturbances. The results of this review, published in Sleep Medicine Reviews, determined that meditation significantly improves both sleep quality and duration, well beyond placebo effects. Researchers pointed out that meditation activates the parts of the brain involved in regulating sleep and decreases arousal levels, thus facilitating falling asleep.

Changes in physiology due to meditation also have a crucial role in the improvement of sleep quality. Neuroimaging and physiological studies indicate that meditation increases activity in the prefrontal cortex, slows brain wave patterns, and reduces cortisol levels, leading to increased relaxation and better sleep. Meditation also improves the secretion of melatonin, an important hormone involved in regulating sleep-wake cycles.

It also finds evidence in research into the autonomic nervous system responsible for bodily functions not controlled by conscious will, such as breathing, heartbeat, and digestion processes. The practices of meditation have been found to positively affect this system by shifting from sympathetic to parasympathetic dominance. This shift reduces the 'fight or flight' response, which is often heightened in individuals with insomnia, and promotes the 'rest and digest' state, which is favorable for sleep.

Among these physiological understandings, psychological benefits such as reduced anxiety and lower levels of stress form an integral part of understanding why meditation improves sleep. Anxiety and stress are common roots of sleep disorders; thus, the ability of meditation to mitigate these elements add to its effectiveness as a sleeping remedy. Minimizing the cognitive and physiological manifestations of stress can create a more relaxed condition that makes falling asleep and having deeper sleeps possible.

Meditation will also be incorporated into potential treatment plans by healthcare professionals, who acknowledge the non-invasive, inexpensive nature, and ease with which such practices can be implemented. Unlike pharmacological interventions, meditation offers no risk of dependency or withdrawal symptoms and, therefore, can be a long-term solution sustainably.

This, therefore, consolidates various research in a compelling case for the inclusion of meditation within public health strategies that deal with sleep disorders; it supports not only the effectiveness of meditation to improve sleep quality but also its potential as a cornerstone for a comprehensive approach to health and well-being.

In developing the above discussion to an understanding of physiological and neurological benefits underlying meditation's impact on sleep, it is evident that it is not a simple symptom relief but rather a profoundly powerful transformational tool able to significantly improve one's quality of life by enhancing sleep quality. This understanding now allows for deeper exploration of how meditation can be tailored to meet individual needs and integrated into one's daily routine for optimal health and well-being.

Meditation's impact on sleep goes far beyond the mere reduction of bedtime anxiety to encompass substantial physiological and neurological benefits that improve both sleep quality and general health. This connection between meditation and sleep involves complex interactions within the brain and the central nervous system, underlining the deep changes these practices can promote.

Central to understanding how meditation affects sleep is its influence on the brain's structure and function. Neuroimaging has indeed documented that during meditation, brain wave activity shifts from higher frequency waves associated with wakefulness to slower and more stable waves, which favor relaxation and sleep. Alpha and theta wave activity increases during meditation; both are associated with relaxed wakefulness and the transition to sleep. It thus primes the mind for sleep and hopefully will increase the amount of deep sleep one experiences.

Secondly, meditation alters several key parts of the brain integral to emotional regulation and control over stress responses: the prefrontal cortex-a part of the brain engaged in decision-making and self-regulation-expresses more activity and connectivity among long-term meditators. Such development mediates activities of the amygdala, which is very active in people suffering from anxiety and stress disorders that interfere with sleep. Thus, meditation decreases the activity of the amygdala and, as a result, stabilizes the emotional activities and reduces the level of stress in general, helping to improve sleep.

Meditation supports other key areas involved in emotion and the forming of memory, such as the hippocampus. This is in a physical sense, too, where meditation has been shown to increase the volume of the hippocampus, thereby enhancing memory but also building up resilience to stress. This can be related to sleep, as improved memory consolidation and reduced stress are both conducive to restful and restorative sleep.

Beyond these neurological changes, meditation also affects the autonomic nervous system in profound ways, controlling the body's involuntary physiological processes, from heartbeat and respiration to digestion. The regular practice of this leads the physiology away from domination by the sympathetic nervous system, known otherwise as the fight-or-flight response, toward parasympathetic dominance, or rest-and-digest. It's important for firing off the body's relaxation response, lowering heart rate and blood pressure, and bringing on deeper breathing-all physiological changes conducive to falling asleep and sleeping well.

Another critical role that meditation can play in improving sleep quality is its effect on the endocrine system. For example, it controls cortisol, which is often produced in excess when a person is undergoing stress. Cortisol acts to disrupt sleep patterns-especially if its levels in the body are high in the evening. By bringing cortisol secretion into a more normal range, sleep cycles become more normal, which greatly helps both the falling asleep and maintenance of sleep throughout the night.

The interaction between meditation and melatonin, which is responsible for sleep and wakefulness, further illustrates physiological benefits of meditation for sleep. In fact, evening meditation practices have been shown to enhance melatonin levels and improve sleep quality and duration. All in all, this increase in melatonin aids in helping an individual fall asleep but at the same time improves sleep quality because of the higher percentage attributed to REM-a stage when, reputedly, dreams and memories, alongside emotional processing, take place.

In addition, meditation contributes to the least possible level of inflammatory processes within an organism, which typically are associated with sleeping poorly and various other health conditions. Chronic inflammation in the body may cause poor sleep and worsen several sleep disorders, including insomnia and sleep apnea. Reduction of inflammation by meditation promotes sound sleep and overall health.

Considering these comprehensive benefits, there is a reason why meditation is not just a viable alternative to more mainstream sleep therapies but often also preferable. Because meditation deals with no pharmaceuticals whatsoever, there's no possibility of dependency or side effects arising from medication-based treatments dealing with sleep disorders. Non-invasive meditation, with its wide spectrum of benefits accruing to both sleep and overall physical and mental health, thus comes out as a very holistic treatment for the modern desire to return to natural health care solutions.

The following discussion compares these benefits against other treatment modalities and describes future research directions that could further establish and broaden our understanding of meditation as a cornerstone of sleep therapy. This exploration will not only illuminate the unique position that meditation occupies in the landscape of sleep treatments but will also bring into view areas where further research could serve to deepen our understanding and application of these ancient practices within modern medical contexts.

Meditation has been on record to play a critical role in improving sleep, with impressive evidence that it is a valid alternative to traditional sleep treatments like pharmacotherapy and behavioral therapy. As we further delve into meditation's place within the broader spectrum of interventions for sleep disorders, it's clear that this practice holds up well against other methods and offers unique benefits essential in our ongoing struggle with insomnia and other sleep-related problems.

For many, medication serves as the first line of treatment in insomnia. These medications are usually sedatives from the class of benzodiazepines or the newer generation of non-benzodiazepine sleep medicines, which are really very effective in inducing quick sleep. However, they present a gamut of side effects that include drowsiness, cognitive impairment, and even dependency and withdrawal problems. More critically, these medications do not treat the root causes of sleep disturbances and are generally recommended for short-term use only, further limiting their usefulness in managing chronic conditions of sleep. In contrast, meditation represents a non-invasive, sustainable approach, free from all pharmacological side effects. Its benefits extend beyond mere symptom management to foster deeper, more restorative sleep. Meditation works by engaging and enhancing the body's natural relaxation responses, thereby mitigating the underlying stress and anxiety that so often fuel sleep disorders. The sustained practice of meditation can gradually reset the body's sleep architecture in ways that medications simply cannot achieve, leading to longer-term improvements in sleep quality and duration.

Behavioral therapies, particularly cognitive-behavioral therapy for insomnia (CBT-I), represent another cornerstone of non-pharmacological sleep disorder treatment. Cognitive-behavioral therapy for insomnia operates on the principle of modification of sleep habits and sleep misconceptions by techniques such as stimulus control, sleep restriction, and relaxation training. However, while CBT-I is highly effective with enduring benefits without the risks of medications, accessibility is relatively limited by the need for trained therapists and multiple in-person sessions. In this respect, meditation has a clear advantage. Once learned, meditation techniques can be practiced independently at any time and without ongoing professional support, making them a highly accessible and cost-effective solution.

Compared with these more traditional therapies, meditation not only has similar efficacy in many cases but also augments their effectiveness when used as an adjunctive therapy. For instance, meditation techniques that could be utilized in the relaxation training component of CBT-I might deepen the relaxation response and hasten the pace of therapeutic gain. Furthermore, the flexibility of meditation as a treatment modality allows individuals to tailor practices to their specific needs, promoting greater personal agency and adherence to therapy over time.

The neurophysiological side effects of meditation also compare favorably with the neurophysiological side effects arising from other treatments. For instance, studies have proven that meditation increases neuroplasticity-that is, the brain's neurophysiological capacity to restructure itself by creating new neural links. This very capacity is one that undergirds not only improved sleep but also improved cognitive functioning and emotional regulation, many of which are disrupted in chronically sleep-deprived subjects.

Looking ahead, there are promising and plentiful meditation research directions in the context of sleep improvement. Further longitudinal studies are needed to better understand the long-term effects of meditation on sleep architecture and which specific aspects of meditation are most beneficial for specific sleep disorders. Of importance, too, is a growing interest in investigating how specific meditation styles-mindfulness-based stress reduction, transcendental meditation, and mindful awareness practices-affect sleep outcomes. The findings will aid in developing meditation recommendations that balance individual needs and preference.

Another very promising direction of investigation is meditation combined with technology. Wearable technology, monitoring physiological responses both while one is meditating and during sleep, offers new avenues for real-time feedback and personalized instructions. Meditation facilitator apps allowing people to practice and track their progress are increasingly sophisticated; they may make meditation more available than ever for those trying to improve their sleep.

With the constantly growing body of evidence supporting the efficacy of meditation, its integration into mainstream medical practice seems inevitable. Health professionals are starting to recognize the value in prescribing meditation as part of holistic treatment plans for sleep disorders. This shift not only considers the limitations and risks associated with traditional treatments but also falls in line with a broader move toward more integrative, patient-centered care.

In the following section, meditation will be applied to personal sleeping practices and discussed in a way that empowers readers to take useful information on how to use this ancient practice to combat modern maladies. The discussion will not only outline the practical steps involved in initiating and maintaining a meditation practice but also explore how variations in individual responses to meditation can be managed to ensure maximum therapeutic outcomes.

Meditation for sleep quality is not about assuming a new habit but integrating a very transformative practice into daily life that can have a huge impact on overall health and well-being. This section explores the practical ways in which individuals can integrate meditation into their daily routines, especially to fight sleeping disorders like insomnia.

Starting a meditation practice can be overwhelming, but the premise is to start simple and build up. For the beginners in meditation, the process initiates by setting aside a few minutes each day for meditation. This could be every morning to set a serene tone for the day, or in the evening as a way to prepare the mind and body for a night of rest. It is supposed to be ideal, but it may differ for each person according to schedule and lifestyle. Consistency is, however, of essence. A regular practice at the same time of the day will condition both body and mind to shut down and go into a relaxed state more easily.

Setting is an important factor that influences meditation practices, particularly when it is used to improve sleep. It should be quiet and comfortable, where nobody will disturb the person. This could be a nook in the bedroom or a particular chair in the living room that one can associate with a quiet time. The ability to minimize external distractions, such as electronic devices, loud noises, or harsh lighting, will also enhance the focus and quality of meditation.

Those who meditate to improve their sleep may find the integration of techniques that encourage relaxation and sleep preparation to be especially useful. Techniques such as guided imagery, where one visualizes a peaceful scene or event, can help shift the mind away from the stressors of the day. Body scan meditations, in which one mentally scans through parts of the body and consciously relaxes them, are effective in relieving physical tension—a common barrier to sleep.

Deep breathing exercises also form an important part of many meditation practices and have a direct impact on the parasympathetic nervous system, controlling the rest and digest response in the body. Techniques such as the 4-7-8 breathing method, where you breathe in for four seconds, hold the breath for seven seconds, and exhale for eight seconds, can significantly reduce anxiety and prepare the body for sleep. These techniques added to one's bedtime routine will transition the body into sleep mode and signal that it is time to wind down and rest.

Another practical way of integrating meditation into a sleep routine is through the use of digital tools and applications. Many apps guide meditations, relaxation sounds, and sleep stories to help someone along in their meditation. These are extremely helpful in cases where someone finds meditation alone difficult or when he prefers structured guidance. At the same time, keeping a check on screen time is better since too much screen exposure at night would be defeating its purpose because of its effect on melatonin through blue light emission.

In practice, the long-term maintenance of any meditation practice requires not only consistency but also creativity and personalization, since the specifics of need and circumstance constantly shift over time. Some people may find that their meditation needs can change from night to night-some nights require a longer meditation to get the tension out, while other nights maybe just a few deep breaths are needed before falling asleep. The development of a skill to listen to one's body and work out at the time one feels suitable is a significant gain in time and with experience. Further, a practice of meditation combined with other healthy lifestyle choices could have an enhancing effect on its benefits. Regular physical activity, a balanced diet, and good sleep hygiene alone improve the quality of sleep, but together with meditation, provide a sound framework for fighting insomnia and improving general health. For those who would like to deepen their practice or investigate other modalities of meditation, there is no shortage of resources. Local meditation classes, workshops, and retreats offer a structured learning environment and a community of support, which may be particularly helpful for a beginner. Books, online courses, and how-to videos may also be helpful in offering key insights and techniques that could further one's practice.

Ultimately, the incorporation of meditation into one's life as a remedy for sleep disturbances is a journey of experimentation, learning, and growth. It requires patience and persistence, as the benefits of meditation accumulate over time. The practice will not only help to improve sleep but also bring better mental clarity, emotional stability, and resilience against stress, leading to a high quality of life.

Meditation Techniques for Better Sleep

Mastery of breathing forms the basis of many meditative practices, especially when the goal is to reduce the anxiety that usually disrupts sleep. In fact, breathing exercises are such important tools that no person desiring better quality sleep through meditation should be without them in their armor. This section now looks at various techniques of breathing that target specifically bedtime anxiety and hence offer a passageway to a more restful and serene night.

Probably one of the best activities that can help reduce bedtime anxiety is the diaphragmatic breathing exercise, popularly known as deep breathing. A conscious, deliberate slowing and deepening of the breath, it encourages full oxygen exchange-the beneficial trade of incoming oxygen for outgoing carbon dioxide. Besides reducing heart rate, this technique also lowers blood pressure, thus fostering a sleep-conducive state. Practitioners are encouraged to lie in their beds and place one hand on the chest and the other on the abdomen to monitor their breaths, ensuring that the diaphragm is doing the work rather than the chest. This tactile feedback is instrumental in helping individuals learn to breathe more deeply and effectively. Another powerful breathing method is the 4-7-8 technique, developed by Dr. Andrew Weil. It's praised for its simplicity and effectiveness in how it lets one feel calm and relaxed. The procedure will be to breathe in quietly through the nose for four seconds, hold the breath for seven seconds, and blow out hard through the mouth for eight seconds. This model works effectively in reducing anxiety since controlled breathing in a rhythmic pattern occupies the mind and saves it from focusing on any stressors of disruption to sleep.

Progressive relaxation breathing is also effective for those getting ready to sleep. The process involves synchronization of breathing in progressive tensing and relaxation of different groups of muscles within the body. This practice relaxes the body and helps in taking your mind off thoughts that breed anxiety. By methodically going through muscle groups-from the toes to the crown of the head-practitioners can achieve a comprehensive state of physical relaxation, which is a way towards sleep.

For those whose minds start racing just as bedtime approaches, one technique that may be beneficial is counting breaths. It includes the slow counting of each exhalation, up to ten, starting over again. The simplicity of counting may quiet the din of anxiety-provoking thoughts by placing the attention of the mind squarely on the process of counting and breathing. If the mind wanders, and it most assuredly will, the injunction is gently to return without judgment to counting. This technique is not only helpful to get into sleep, but also it is very useful to get back into sleep after midnight awakenings.

The effect of visualization added to breathing can be extended further. This is commonly known as guided imagery. Here, one visualizes an imaginary, peaceful place or scenario along with deep breathing. Whether it is a quiet beach at sunset, a tranquil path through the forest, or any other place of serenity, visualization keeps one's mind focused on the peaceful pictures with the rhythmic pattern of breathing slowly and deep. This technique taps into the sensory memory for sights, sounds, and scents of places associated with relaxation, actually taking the practitioner away from the stressors of the day into a sleep-conducive state. Another rather subtle approach is that of alternate nostril breathing, which finds its roots deeply embedded in the yogic tradition. This consists of covering one nostril and then breathing through the other, shifting with each breath to the other nostril. This not only focuses the mind but also balances the left and right hemispheres of the brain, inducing mental clarity and calm. By incorporating a tactile element-the touch of a finger closing off a nostril-it provides a physical anchor for the mind, further aiding in the reduction of pre-sleep anxiety.

These breathing techniques, other than reducing anxiety when constantly done at bedtime, signal to the body that sleep is in order. This acts as a cue or trigger that the day has come to an end, and rest is near, since they are part of a ritual the body learns to recognize by repeating it over time. Besides, these exercises can easily be combined with body scan meditations, further enhancing the effect of relaxation, since the body is already primed for deep relaxation and the mind attuned to the inward focus. Together, they forge a powerful alliance in battling insomnia and form a bridge to the subsequent techniques discussed in this book, which involve physical relaxation of the body for preparing to sleep.

The journey to restful sleep through meditation often involves many turns, but there are indeed ways, among which body scan meditations turn out to be most effectual in physically relaxing the body before sleep. This will involve the sequential mental scanning of the body from head to toe or vice versa, observing sensations without trying to change them. This is done to bridge the gap between the body and the mind, preparing them for sleep by becoming aware and relaxed.

Body scan meditation is also a basic procedure in mindfulness meditation to create a heightened state of body awareness. It allows the practitioner to be sensitive to all physical sensations in each part of the body, usually from the toes upwards. Each part of the body is noted in the mind and then freed from tension, often along with controlled, deep breathing. Such a progress is useful to highlight and release any hidden pockets of tension that often are not felt in daily hustles and interfere with the falling asleep or further going into deeper stages of sleep.

It will not only be a means of relaxation but also a method of cultivating mindfulness, since the practitioner learns to observe and release thoughts, feelings, and physical sensations that might contribute to stress and insomnia. This systematic shifting of attention through different areas of the body trains the mind to focus on the present and detach from the day's worries and planning that often invade the hours of pre-sleep and disturb rest.

Besides, the practice of body scan meditation has been shown to significantly enhance parasympathetic nervous system activity, or the part of the autonomic nervous system responsible for 'rest and digest' activities. In this process, the body is coaxed into a state of relaxation, heart rate and blood pressure drop, and the brain releases neurotransmitters that promote calm and sleep. This physiological shift can be palpable and a potent antidote to the symptoms of insomnia, which often include a hyper-aroused physiological state.

Practically, this may be done lying down-this is ideal for those preparing for sleep-and the environment should support relaxation, perhaps dimly lit and free from noise and distractions. As the scan continues, the practitioner is to imagine that the breath is reaching each part, soothing and softening muscles. The fact is that this might deepen the relaxation experience and create a profound habit of being mindfully attentive to bodily sensations, translating into more ease while falling asleep.

Attention to all parts in such detail serves to guarantee that no area with accumulated tension goes unnoticed. Starting from the toes, the arches of the feet, ankles, and upward through the legs, one observes and relaxes each portion. The journey continues upward through the torso, back, arms, and up into the shoulders-a common repository for daily stress. This often trickles down through the neck, jaw, and facial muscles, too, as conscious relaxation of these areas can greatly affect overall levels of stress and anxiety.

This has usually brought on, as it progresses to the head, a great release of the more general tension, with increasing sensations of heaviness and warmth in the body--indicative of the preparation of sleep. This may continue into the guided visualizations, whereby the disposition towards sleep of the mind may be taken further by creating imagery within the mind that would do further to induce relaxation and sleep.

Guided visualizations very often follow naturally after the body scan meditations in sleep therapy. While the latter mainly deals with physical sensations and relaxations, guided visualizations introduce soothing, serene images to the mind's eye, which encourage the mind to let go of stressful thoughts and slip into a sleep-conducive state. The association of the body's physical relaxation with, subsequently, the engagement of the mind with peaceful and sleep-conducive imagery will go a long way toward improving sleep quality, especially in cases where insomnia is compounded by anxiety and rumination.

The movement from body scan meditation to guided visualizations signifies a holistic approach to sleep meditation, engaging in the physical and mental dimensions of relaxation. This comprehensively prepares not just the body for sleep but also stages a serene introduction for the mind to follow, amalgamating the benefits of meditation fully into the sleep preparation process. This technique thus aids not only in the swiftness of falling asleep but also in the attainment of a deeper and more restorative sleep state, which is important for health and wellness.

Among these techniques and tools for sleep promotion and insomnia management, guided imagery has a significant place. This technique employs imagination to attain a relaxed state and might be especially helpful for people whose minds tend to race or those who are burdened with anxiety as bedtime approaches. In other words, a guided visualization is intended, by its very nature, to shift the focus of a person's mind away from daily stresses and concerns unto calming, serene images and scenarios, hence creating the sleep-conducive environment. Guided visualization involves bringing peaceful, vivid images up in the mind's eye. These could be visualizations of a place, real or imagined, in which a person feels totally at ease: a quiet beach at sunset, a cool path in the forest, or even just a cozy, crackling fireside. What matters is that the imagery is directed to all of one's senses, providing an experience which completely absorbs the mind and lulls it to sleep. Practitioners may be invited to pay attention to the sensation of the warmth of the sun on the skin, to the sounds of waves caressing the shore, perhaps to fresh pine aromas, or to the touch that an armchair provides upon sitting. Such a multisensory approach will help in gaining effective distraction from mundane anxiety or engaging the parasympathetic nervous system to brake their heart rate and relax body muscles.

Guided visualizations not only help to tranquilize the mind, but also normalize emotions. For many people, bedtime is a particular moment when stresses of the day come to the lead of thought, which is absolutely difficult to dismiss. The more one redirects focus on calming images, the lesser the production of cortisol, the stress hormone, making it easier to sleep. Such practices can train the mind more easily to let go of anxiety and fall into this peaceful state, which is much needed for falling asleep as well as maintaining deep sleep throughout the night.

This technique can also be very helpful for those who have conditions like PTSD, where intrusive thoughts and hyperarousal are very common. Guided visualizations provide a safe haven for the mind-a controlled and comforting space that stands in contrast to the chaos of anxiety and fear. This can be especially powerful before sleep, when such conditions can become more pronounced in the quiet and stillness.

The practice can be guided either by a recording or by a live guide. In either case, a soft, soothing voice guides the practitioner through the scenes, often first by guiding the participant in deep breathing exercises to start them off into a state of relaxation. The narrative can then shift into the visualization, guiding the participant through various sensory experiences associated with the relaxing scene. As the scenario continues, the person is taken further into the environment to become more involved, enhancing feelings of peace and relaxation.

Guided visualizations incorporated into a bedtime routine can really work wonders in improving sleep quality. This is indeed a very flexible technique, and it is easy to tailor to suit individual tastes and requirements. Some people find one scenario more soothing than others, and exploration of options will be essential in finding what really works best. Furthermore, the practice may get more effective as time goes on because one's mind will get so used to the response needed to be induced into this state of relaxation by guided imagery.

This form of relaxation also works well with other meditation and mindfulness practices for improving sleep. For example, following up a body scan with a guided visualization can enhance the overall relaxation experience, easing the body and then the mind into a sleep-ready state. Similarly, combining these visualizations with mindfulness or meditation apps that provide background sounds or music can amplify the immersive experience, making the practice even more effective.

Directions in research and application alike are auspicious for guided visualizations to continue their expansion in a role in holistic sleep therapies. Innovations in virtual reality, for example, create new opportunities for delivering more immersive forms of guided visualizations, which could heighten the efficacy. This, however, will continue to get even better as research is continually evolving our understanding of how best this tool can be utilized against insomnia for even more advanced techniques and refined approach toward restful sleep for increased numbers of individuals.

Guided visualizations represent the epitome in a relaxed effort to sink into the nooks of sleep. In more ways than one, this is an effective means of detaching from stress at the end of a day to engage in a recuperative practice that enhances quality: both in sleep, and the feeling of well-being throughout an individual's day. Incorporating this practice into better sleeping hygiene provides one with yet another more natural way to fight nighttime sleep difficulties without dependency on pharmaceutical drugs.

Creating a Conducive Sleep Environment

A sleeping sanctuary is a must to get perfect nightly sleep. Sleep surroundings can either distress your ability to quickly fall asleep or have long, continuous sleeps. The well-designed sleep space thoughtfully promotes all the physiological events involved in sleep and signals the brain that it's time for winding down to go into a rest mode. Here are a few helpful suggestions that will help in transforming the bedroom into the perfect place for sleeping-and with it, an environment for restful sleep.

Aesthetics: Colors, decoration, and general design in the room need to be selected according to the theme of giving out a peaceful and very tranquil atmosphere. Soft, subdued color schemes, such as blues, greens, and earth tones, are said to be soothing to the mind and help drive away anxiety and stress. These colors are preferred over bright bold colors, which might stir up the brain and get a person alert. Besides, clutter should be avoided. A neat and uncluttered environment reduces anxiety and distractions, hence making it easier to relax at the end of the day.

The choice of bedding and sleep accessories is related to the quality of sleep. So, one should invest in a very good-quality mattress and pillows that support one's preferred sleeping position and ensure that the spine is aligned properly. A good mattress could make all the difference in comfort during sleep and may help prevent pain and discomfort that wakes one up anytime during the night. Moreover, choose bedding materials that are well-ventilated and pleasant to the skin. Natural fibers like cotton, bamboo, or linen tend to breathe well and regulate your sleeping temperature all night long.

Light control is also an important feature of sleep sanctuary design. More than anything, the light, especially blue light coming from screens, suppresses the secretion of melatonin, a hormone signaling your body that it's time to sleep. Lend your bedroom a pair of blackout curtains or heavy drapes to block outside light, and try not to use electronic devices in the bedroom. If you are using your phone or other devices before bed, placing them on "night mode" reduces the amount of blue light coming from these devices. This can help minimize this problem.

Sound is another factor that can be greatly affect sleep quality. Noises can disrupt your sleep stage, making your sleep less restful. If you are living in a noisy area, soundproofing your room can effectively protect you from disrupting sounds. Another way is to use the white noise machine or an app that can mask outside sounds with the soothing patter of rain, wind, or waves of the sea; this helps when the complete silence keeps people awake. Next up is your sleeping environment's temperature. The ideal temperature for sleep is around 65 degrees Fahrenheit (ca. 18 °C), as cooler temperatures help lower the body's core temperature, signaling that it's time to sleep. Ensure your room is equipped with a thermostat that allows for precise temperature control. This can be achieved by keeping them cool with fans or air conditioning during the warmer months; in the colder months, it will require adequate bedding and adjustments in heating to avoid cold conditions.

It's good for lights to be soft, using low wattage or indirect lighting to aid relaxation. Harsh overhead lights shock the body, as it interferes with the release of melatonin in the body. The dimmers or putting soft and warm bulbs in your lamp could adjust the light, especially at evening time to begin getting ready for bed; just like nature's waning sun tells your system night is near.

Beyond these physical aspects, the scent of your room can affect the quality of your sleep. The soothing effects from aromatherapy can be induced with the use of scented essential oils, such as lavender, chamomile, or sandalwood. These scents can be introduced by diffusers, spritzed on linens, or used in bath products as part of a presleep routine.

Creating a sleep-conducive environment is very personal, and what works for A might not work for B. It is about fiddling around and trying out arrangements and adjustments to see what helps you the most in your relaxation towards sleep. With these tips considered and modified according to your preference, you can create a haven for yourself to get quality restful sleep night after night.

Setting up an optimal sleep environment involves an understanding of how light, sound, and temperature interrelate with sleep quality. Each one of these components is significant in regulating our circadian rhythms, which are the natural internal processes that cycle between states of sleep and wakefulness and repeat approximately every 24 hours.

Light: Exposure to light is perhaps the most significant external factor that affects sleep. It affects the production of melatonin, a hormone that dictates the sleep-wake cycles of our body. While natural light regulates our circadian rhythm, agreeing with the ambient environment, artificial lighting in the evening completely disrupts this process. The blue light from screens on smartphones, computers, and televisions is particularly disrupting because it signals the brain to lower melatonin production, which can delay sleep onset and reduce sleep quality.

It is worth noting that reducing the use of screens for at least an hour before bedtime may help diminish the impact of blue light. Alternatively, using apps or settings that filter out blue light can also help. Blackout curtains or shades can be installed in the bedroom to block out the unnecessary external light, including streetlamps and vehicle headlights, that may interfere with sleeping. Dim red lights used for night lights are helpful if a person needs some light at nighttime for safe movement around. Red light has the least power to shift the circadian rhythm and suppress melatonin.

Sound: Noises can totally disrupt sleep, though the degree can vary widely among individuals. Some may find even the slightest noise disruptive, while others may not be as sensitive. Intermittent and high-decibel sounds such as traffic noise, dogs barking, or even a snoring partner disrupt the cycles of sleep, leading to fragmented sleep and poor quality thereof. On the other hand, low-level white noise of constant character masks the disturbing sounds and may even have a soothing effect. The sound machines or fans many people use create a steady, predictable sound that helps mask disturbing noises and becomes part of a bedtime routine that tells the body it's time to sleep.

Temperature: The body's core temperature needs to drop slightly to initiate sleep, which is why cooler room temperatures are generally more conducive to sleep. Most experts recommend setting your bedroom temperature around 65 degrees Fahrenheit (ca. 18 °C), but personal preferences can vary. The key is to keep the temperature not so cold that it wakes you, yet not so warm that it prevents your body temperature from lowering adequately to induce sleep. Wearing breathable bedding and sleepwear can also help maintain a comfortable sleeping temperature throughout the night.

You would enhance both the quality and quantity of your sleep if there is proper balance between light, sound, and temperature in your bedroom. This balance not only allows the person to fall asleep much faster, but also maintains better and deeper sleep cycles that make sleep more restorative.

In transitioning these environmental factors toward a bedroom optimized for meditation and sleep, a few additional considerations can be made. The space should be inviting and clutter-free, since it could unconsciously signal chaos to the brain and inhibit relaxation. It may also include elements such as comfortable seating or cushions to meditate on, or even an area for practice if space allows. Additionally, consider incorporating calming scents, such as lavender or chamomile, through candles or essential oils to help signal to your body that it is time to wind down and prepare for sleep.

By adjusting these aspects of your sleep environment, you not only foster conditions that are conducive to sleep but also create a serene space that supports both meditation and relaxation, ultimately enhancing overall well-being.

It is much more than just aesthetically changing your bedroom into a sanctuary for sleep and meditation; it is a strategic process that combines comfort, functionality, and tranquility in a manner that will offer the right atmosphere for relaxation and restorative sleep. This should be a space that will help one sleep but also improve the quality of meditation. First, consider the physical layout of the room. Place your bed in a natural, relaxed position. Some people like having their bed facing the door because it makes them feel safer and more comfortable. The bed should look inviting and comfortable. Buy a good mattress, which would suit your body type and sleeping style-be it a side sleeper, back, or stomach sleeper. Pair this with pillows that support your neck and head properly.

Equally, appealing is the choice of bedding. Go for natural fibers such as cotton, bamboo, or linen. The latter breathe better compared to synthetic materials and act well in regulating body temperature through the night. Choose sheets, blankets, and comforters that feel good on the skin, since tactile comfort means a lot when aiming for relaxation. The color of your bedding can also affect your mood; soothing colors like pastels, light blues, greens, and grays are known to help reduce stress and induce calmness.

Beyond the bed, lighting in your bedroom is an important factor. Being exposed to too much light before bed upsets your circadian rhythm and the production of melatonin, a hormone that makes one sleep. Dimmable lights are ideal for a bedroom used for meditation and sleep, where changes in light can easily make the right ambiance. If you live in an area with a lot of nighttime light pollution, install blackout curtains or heavy shades to block out outside light. An eye mask can be an effective and simple solution.

Another important aspect is good sound management. For meditation or sleeping, a quiet environment helps much. If there is a noise disturbance from outside, the room should be soundproof; one can also use machinery to create white noise and cover the disturbing sounds through this, or use a fan instead. Soft, rhythmic sounds can also be implemented as an accompaniment in meditation practices, helping along gentle music or nature sounds as the mind goes even further into a deeper depth of relaxation.

Temperature control plays a pivotal role in sleep quality. The ideal bedroom temperature for most people is about 65 degrees Fahrenheit (ca. 18 °C), but this can vary based on personal preference. Ensure your heating or cooling system is adjusted accordingly before bedtime to maintain a comfortable sleeping environment. A programmable thermostat can automate this process, adjusting the room temperature in preparation for your bedtime.

Creating a dedicated space for meditation within your bedroom can significantly enhance your practice. This doesn't need to be large; even a small corner of the room can be transformed into a meditative space with the addition of a comfortable chair or cushion, a small table for candles or incense, and perhaps some inspirational items like statues, crystals, or artwork that resonates with your spiritual practice.

Organization and cleanliness of the bedroom also matter. Clutter around makes for cluttered brains, which is undoubtedly what one would rather not experience during meditation and asleep. Regularly declutter your space to maintain order and peace. This includes the cable and electronic device management. Keep them to the barest minimum to avoid distractions.

Finally, add some sensory elements that may appeal to your senses and promote relaxation. Aromatherapy with the use of scents such as lavender or chamomile is said to have calming effects. Light tactile elements like plush rugs or soft throws can make the space feel safer and more comforting.

By thoughtfully designing your bedroom for sleeping and meditation, you are not only creating a functional and beautiful space, but also a personal retreat that nurtures health and well-being. This kind of thoughtfulness in design ensures that every night and each meditation session inside those walls is channeled into deeper relaxation and rejuvenation for better mental, physical, and emotional health.

Integrating Meditation into Your Nightly Routine

This would bring a radical change in the ability to sleep easily and soundly, through the establishment of a pre-sleep meditation routine. The key is really to create a sequence that will transition you from being busy in your day to the calmness needed to rest well. This involves cultivating a series of rituals that signal to your body and mind that it's time to wind down and prepare for the night. Here's a detailed guide to crafting a meditation routine that can be seamlessly integrated into your nightly regimen.

Start by setting the same time daily for meditation, preferably between 30 and 60 minutes before retiring to bed. Because consistency regulates your body's sleep-wake cycle. Gradually, this regular timing will automatically trigger the sleeping mechanism in your system, and thus it will be easy to catch sleep after meditation.

The environment in which you meditate plays a big role in your practice. Find a quiet, comfortable spot in your home that you can dedicate to your night ritual. It could be a corner in your bedroom or any other area that can be associated with relaxation and tranquility. Equip this room with items that can heighten the tranquility of the ambiance through soft lighting, sitting chairs or even a meditation cushion, or nature elements like plants and perhaps a small fountain.

When your space is set, you do a pre-meditation ritual to transition yourself from the active part of your day to the more reflective part. This can be a series of gentle stretches or yoga poses that help your body understand this is a time to slow down. You can also use this time to engage in a short reading of meditation-focused literature or inspirational texts that will focus your thoughts inward.

Begin your meditation by focusing first on your breath. Deep, rhythmic breathing is a potent tool for minimizing stress and bringing one's awareness to the present moment. Begin with the 4-7-8 breathing technique: inhale for four counts, hold your breath for seven counts, and exhale slowly for eight counts. This technique is especially effective in calming the nervous system and sharpening focus.

After centering yourself with deep breathing, transition into either a guided visualization or a body scan meditation. For the latter, methodically focus your attention on different parts of your body, starting from your toes and moving upward, letting each conscious part of your body relax. Visualize the tension melting away with every exhalation. This will soothe your body and quiet your mind in preparation for sleep.

Practice mindfulness meditation-not holding onto any thought. Allow the mind to notice each thought that comes into your head and then gently release it, bringing your focus back to your breath or body. This helps detach the person from the mental chatter and day's worries that usually avoid sleep.

Deepen the sensation of relaxation for your meditation using soothing sounds or sleep music. Sounds like slow, soft melodies, or nature sounds such as rain or ocean waves, can serve to further deepen the relaxation effects of your meditation process. Close your meditation session with one minute of gratitude. Reflect on your day and acknowledge little things that you are grateful for. This positive reflection nurtures feelings of contentment and peace, further aligning your mind and body toward restful sleep.

As you complete your practice, keep the peace and take that peace with you into bedtime. Keep the lighting low and activities quiet. Avoid screens and other stimulants that may disturb the tranquility you have built. Instead, continue with soothing activities, such as reading a book or briefly journaling about your meditation experience or thoughts that came up during your practice.

It then links the meditation act into your nightly routine as a ritual that not only will work on improving sleep quality, but also in fostering a better relationship with rest, in general. With time, this will become more than just a cue to fall asleep; it will be that protected part of your daily routine for peace, with its positive effects on mental and physical well-being.

Meditation is a powerful bridge between the hustle of the day and the quiet of the night, serving as a method to transition with poise from the activities of daily living to the rest and relaxation of a night's sleep. By setting up meditation to close out your day, you set in motion a night of restorative sleep that helps recreate a natural rhythm between times of wakefulness and times of rest, further contributing to overall quality sleep and ease into sleep.

First, to effectively use meditation as a transitional tool, it's helpful to understand that meditation doesn't have to be some long or laborious process. The goal is to make a buffer zone between your daily stressors and sleep time, wherein you can unload the mental burdens and physical tension of the day before lying down to rest. This may be achieved with simple, focused practices that help stabilize your mind and relax your body.

Set a specific time every evening for your transition period. This has to be a time when you can commit consistently to unwind, and it is better if it is 30 to 45 minutes before sleeping. Consistency in any sleep hygiene practice strengthens the internal clock of your body and prepares your system for rest at the right time.

Begin this period by turning off the lights in your living room and turning off all electronic devices emitting blue light, such as TVs, computers, and smartphones. It is documented that blue light suppresses melatonin secretion, a hormone responsible for sending sleep signals to your body. This would help your body, by lowering this light, to be more effective in the preparation of sleep.

Now, do a simple seated meditation practice. Find a quiet place to sit where you will not be disturbed. Sit comfortably in a position on a cushion on the floor or in a chair, keeping your back straight but not tense. Take a few deep, slow breaths to let your body know that it's time to slow down. Take deep breaths through your nose, hold for a few seconds, and exhale very slowly through your mouth. Do this several times, paying attention only to your breathing.

As you settle into this rhythm of breathing, begin to let your mind make the transition from active thinking about the events of the day to a more reflective and observant state. Note the thoughts that come into your head; acknowledge their presence, then let them go, returning your focus each time to your breath. This helps in letting go of stresses of the day and bringing your mind to center in the present moment.

It would also be an opportunity for deeper meditation: observe with mindfulness, observe your body, and listen to all the different sounds around without judgment-the sensation of the breath in your nostrils or leaving it, the press of your weight downwards into your seat, perhaps distant noise of the traffic, or wind. The only thing that keeps your awareness anchored into the present is not slipping your mind backward into the concerns of today or forward into the worries of tomorrow.

Progressive muscle relaxation is another great method that works wonders during the transition phase. Actively release all the muscles in your body, starting from the bottom up, starting with your toes. As you inhale, tense the muscle; hold a few seconds, then exhale, releasing the tension and visualizing stress and fatigue leaving your body. This soothes the nervous system and prepares your body for deep rest.

As you work your way out of a meditation session, take a few minutes and sit silently or reflect on whatever you feel grateful for; reflect upon the things during the day that you appreciate. Such positive recapsulation may transform your mindset from stressful to one of fulfillment, which has been shown to offer relaxation and improve sleep.

Lastly, as you transition from meditation to sleep, let everything be in that relaxed mode. You should also avoid stimulating activities right after meditation. Continue with the serenity by probably reading a light book under soft light, listening to soft music, or doing some light stretches or yoga poses that tell your body it's time to hit the sack.

By making meditation a part of your nightly routine and using it as a transition tool, you bridge the gap between day and night quite nicely, letting your mind and body move into sleep mode more naturally and with ease. This will help improve not only the quality of your sleep but also contribute to your overall well-being by giving you a quiet and reflective end to your day.

While meditation does indeed yield great improvements in sleep and reduction of stress, there are some obstacles the newcomer and the seasoned practitioner alike may be faced with that can detract from its effectiveness. Understanding them and having a strategy for overcoming them can improve your meditation and ensure it continues to play an enriching role in your nighttime routine.

Among the common issues many confront is the one dealing with focusing. Distractions-both external noises and internal thoughts-can get in the way of meditation. The mind will wander, which is not a sign of bad meditation. When that happens, instead of feeling frustrated, acknowledge the distraction and softly bring your attention back to your focal point, whether your breath, a specific mantra, or sensations within your body. This practice of returning your focus is actually where much of the benefit of meditation occurs, as it trains the brain to maintain control over attention and fosters a greater sense of mental clarity.

Physical discomfort is another frequent challenge. Sitting in one position for the duration of a meditation session can lead to stiffness or pain in various parts of the body. For this, keep in mind that your meditation posture should be sustainable. You do not have to sit cross-legged if that feels uncomfortable; you may use supportive cushions, sit on a chair, or even lie down. What is important in this regard is to maintain a posture which allows for balanced alignment of the body without straining any part. Additionally, make small adjustments as needed during your practice to relieve discomfort, always returning to a state of physical stillness with minimal movement to maintain the meditative state.

Drowsiness can also pose a significant barrier, especially when meditating to aid sleep. It might seem beneficial to feel sleepy if you're preparing for bed, but falling asleep during meditation can become a habit that undermines the practice of mindfulness. Counteract this by trying to meditate in a slightly cool room, which will help to keep you alert. Or, if meditating later in the evening, try scheduling meditation for earlier in the evening and not right before bedtime, or use more active meditation styles, such as walking meditation or mindful movement, to stay alert.

Another frustration pertains to impatience if the desired results do not seem to manifest in reasonably quick order. Benefits from meditation can be experienced after some time, especially those related to sleep improvement. You should approach meditation as a process in which you want to focus on the journey rather than the destination. You can celebrate small accomplishments when you notice that your mind wandered less than usual during that session or you feel a little more relaxed than other times. The key to deeper benefits is in continued practice; just keep to your schedule and be patient with persistence.

Many also find it difficult to maintain a regular schedule, which is crucial for meditation to positively affect sleep. The demands of life can make it challenging to carve out time every day for meditation. Address this by incorporating meditation into your schedule as a fixed part of your bedtime routine, much like brushing your teeth or taking a bath. Consistency enhances not only the effectiveness of meditation but also the habit, making it a natural part of nightly wind-down.

For those who are overwhelmed with where to start or how to progress in their practice, guided meditations can be super helpful. These will provide a structured meditation experience ideal for beginners or people who have trouble focusing. Many apps and online platforms offer guided sessions that will help you understand the basics of meditation, provide a variety in meditation styles, and keep the practice interesting.

The third and last one would be skepticism, which could result from preconceived notions about what meditation is or doubts about its scientific support. Studying neuroscientific research into the benefits of meditation in cognition and emotional regulation helps reaffirm its validity. Support through a community of meditators or consulting a meditation teacher will provide greater depth in understanding and commitment.

In conclusion, though you may be faced with numerous challenges in your meditation practice, the ability to recognize common problems and apply strategies to help overcome them can greatly facilitate your use of meditation as an effective tool for enhancing sleep and overall well-being. With time and practice, meditation can become a seamless and invaluable part of your life, offering profound benefits that extend far beyond the meditation cushion.

Advanced Meditation Practices

Deepening your meditation over time is not just about the length of time you spend in meditation, but it's also about deepening mindfulness and the depth of experiences. As you continue to get used to sitting in meditation, you start to realize that there is a great deal of technique you can use to improve your meditation practice and establish a deeper connection between meditative state and daily life; this can greatly enhance quality sleep.

To meditate more deeply, first refine your focus. For a beginning practitioner, the goal may simply be to sustain concentration for a certain period of time. As one advances, however, the emphasis of the practice should shift toward achieving a deeper state of inner stillness and silence. This can be facilitated by focusing on more subtle objects of meditation, such as the sensation of breath entering and leaving the nostrils rather than simply the rise and fall of the chest or abdomen. This finer point of focus sharpens your concentration and brings a deeper tranquility that permeates both mind and body, setting a foundation for improved sleep.

Another great practice for deepening meditation is progressive relaxation. Starting at one end of the body, it works progressively through each muscle group, letting go of tense muscles. This method relaxes deeper in meditation but also has the benefit of recognition and dissolving of physical tension in preparation for sleep.

Smoothen your meditation exercises with visualization techniques. These are imaginations of a serene setting or some tranquilizing sequence of events. This is particularly helpful before bed, as it gets the mind tuned for a smooth transition to sleep. In such a manner, by vividly imagining a tranquil scene-like quiet beach at sunset or soft rainfall in a lush forest-you're engaging the mind at deeper levels than a simple form of relaxation to encourage one to dive more deeply into tranquility. Other powerful tools to deepen meditation include the repetition of mantras. A mantra can be a word, phrase, or sound that is repeated during meditation to help focus and quiet the mind. The repetition of a mantra can help ward off distracting thoughts and anchor you in the present moment, making the mind more attuned to the meditative process and less likely to wander at night, thus easing into sleep.

Movement meditation, such as yoga or walking meditation, may be especially helpful for individuals who find it difficult to sit still. These are exercises in which movement is combined with meditation to foster mindfulness and also prepare one's body for sleep. Gentle physical activity will release endorphins, decrease stress, and help reduce latency to sleep.

Those who are keen to explore meditation's spiritual dimensions may find it interesting to look into different traditions and their meditation practices. Zen meditation, Vipassana, and transcendental meditation are some of the techniques that offer different approaches and insights that could further one's understanding and experience of personal meditation practice and its effects on sleep.

As your meditation practice deepens, it is also beneficial to extend mindfulness beyond designated meditation times. Integrating mindfulness into daily activities—like eating, walking, or even during work—helps maintain a calm, alert state throughout the day, easing anxiety and improving the ability to fall asleep at night.

Lastly, a meditation journal is an invaluable tool on your journey. Writing down experiences, challenges, and the feelings arising during and after meditation will provide insight into patterns and progress. Over time, this record may yield profound insights into how meditation affects your thoughts and emotions, helping to tailor your practice to better address your needs, particularly in relation to sleep.

With these advanced techniques, your meditation practice can evolve from some simple routine into a profound exploration of the mind and consciousness. This deepening in practice enhances not only immediate benefits arising from meditation but also solidifies long-term improvements in quality of sleep and general well-being to make each successive night even more restorative.

Not a practice but a habit of mindfulness in every sphere of activity during the day transforms all our interactions, perceptions, and reactions that crucially influence nighttime sleep quality. This continuum thread would fine-tune the focused mind, quiet down the nervous system, and reduce stress, which all become necessarily required to bring in change in sleep. Through the incorporation of mindfulness during activities, the mind learns serenity, which flows into our sleep, enabling us to let go of the turmoil experienced throughout the day with ease and fall deep into our sleep.

Setting a precedent for one's day with mindfulness can, in fact, set the ground for the rest of one's day. Meditating in the morning-even for a few minutes-can set a calm bar for the rest of your day. It's about taking the time to sit quietly, notice your breath, and set your intention for the day. Not only does it clear the mind, but it also trains the mind to continue this clarity and calm throughout the day. Where practiced regularly, this type of morning meditation may lower the chances of building stress in the body and head during the day, hence giving them an easier night's sleep.

Throughout the day, mindfulness can be interwoven into normal activities, such as eating, walking, or driving to and from work. Mindful eating involves paying full attention to the experience of eating: observing the colors, textures, flavors, and smells of your food, and noticing the sensations of fullness and satisfaction. This helps tune into hunger cues and may prevent overeating, which often leads to discomfort and disrupts sleep.

Mindful walking, whether during a work break or after dinner, is especially helpful. Mindful walking involves a person walking while being very much present, feeling the earth under the feet, noticing breaths, and observing all this without judgment. Not only does this break the loop of continuous sitting, but also minimizes the gathering of stress, paving the way for better sleep.

Moreover, the inclusion of small mindfulness gaps into one's daily work cycle will avoid stress and fatigue accumulation. Every hour, spend several minutes with your eyes closed, breathe deeply, and observe your thoughts without involvement. Those are the small reset buttons that will contribute to the cortisol level lowering and that will not interfere with your sleep later on. Mindfulness also applies to our habits related to technology. Setting boundaries is key in a world where screens dominate our attention. Practice mindfulness in the use of devices by turning off notifications for lengths of time, designating specific times to check emails or social media, and not using screens for at least an hour before bed. This not only minimizes the amount of blue light exposure that interferes with melatonin production but also decreases the mental stimulation that may keep the mind racing during night hours.

In personal interactions, mindfulness encourages a more thoughtful and calm response pattern. By being present in conversations, listening actively, and responding without haste, we minimize misunderstandings and conflicts that may come later and destroy our peace of mind. A practice of attentive listening and speaking helps to nurture relationships that are harmonious and less stressful.

Another great way to incorporate mindfulness into daily life is through journaling. This helps to process what happened during the day by writing down thoughts, experiences, and feelings every evening, which lessens the mental load of the events. Besides helping to clear the mind before sleep, journaling enhances self-awareness and problem-solving, making the anxiety that interferes with sleep less likely to occur.

Finally, gratitude is another powerful mindfulness practice that enhances well-being. Take some time every evening to reflect on the things you are thankful for. It shifts your focus away from problems and stressors toward the positive, and has been linked to better sleep due to enhanced calmness and lower levels of stress.

Practice mindfulness during the day for better waking hours, which will further enhance your quality of sleep. This state of mindful awareness, when continued, keeps us calm and centered, and the unwinding at night becomes much easier, allowing transition into the deep, restorative sleep so much easier. More one practices these methods, the more positive and calm a cycle we go through daily and nightly, which basically shows that the true power of mindfulness is not in times of stillness but rather in weaving every part of our life together seamlessly.

The meditation retreats are pretty changing for those who have disturbed sleep, as it might help in giving their sleeping habit a big reset-a deep sleep and continuous cycle. These retreats create an intensive environment of mindfulness and meditation, away from day-to-day distractions and daily life stressors that generally disturb our sleep quality. The course, through intensive practice, may help participants learn to use meditation as a therapeutic aid that will make a marked difference in their sleep regimen.

Meditation retreats are conducted in peaceful places, like a secluded woodland, countryside, or near tranquil waters. This setting itself is a situation that naturally encourages relaxation, detaching one from the frantic pace of life. Leaving behind the constant barrage of stimuli and demands, the retreat attendees can focus entirely on their mental and physical well-being, which is conducive to resetting natural sleep rhythms.

In meditation retreats, the schedule helps meditators maintain a very specific discipline of regular times to go to bed and to get up in the morning-a very vital factor in correcting odd sleeping habits. Many meditation sessions during the day, most beginning early in the morning, help people not just get deeper into meditation practices but also get their circadian rhythms set correctly, which is absolutely vital for sleeping. Early morning meditation starts the process of wakefulness at the same time each day, while evening meditation relaxes the mind for rest, thus improving sleep quality. There are many types of meditation that are being practiced in retreats, but all these forms have one common objective: to enhance mindfulness and decrease stress, both important elements for a good sleep. Techniques such as guided imagery, progressive relaxation, and mindful breathing are common features that directly address the physiological and psychological aspects of insomnia. For instance, guided imagery may take the mind to a peaceful place, which is a significant contrast to the tossing and turning of a sleepless night. Progressive relaxation techniques systematically relax different muscle groups, releasing tension that might otherwise keep someone awake.

Most retreats also combine sleep hygiene teachings by giving practical tips on routines that support the induction of better sleep. These teachings might touch on how diet affects sleep, the essence of physical activities, and how to maintain a restful environment. In this regard, detailed guidance is provided to make sure that do the participants meditate and learn holistic lifestyle modifications to improve sleep.

A major feature of such retreats is a reduction in screen time. Participants are often encouraged, if not compelled, to disconnect their digital devices. Such avoidance of screens reduces the negative impact of blue light on melatonin production, a hormone important in regulating sleep. The natural increase in melatonin levels, due to the reduction in screen time, helps reset the body's sleep-wake cycle for further improvement in sleep quality.

Besides that, those on meditation retreats also like the company of it. It is easy to be driven by being with others around them focused on the same direction-to become better psychologically and physically. In addition to being comforting, this group dynamic also reminds one about their commitments and practices learned to help sustain it after their retreat is over.

Indeed, many people report, after a retreat, a remarkable improvement in their sleep pattern of falling asleep and sleeping right through the night. The immersive experience of a retreat provides the tools and the understanding necessary to maintain a meditation practice that continues to support sleep health. Skills, habits, and insights acquired in such an intensive and supportive environment can have long-lasting effects on the sleep patterns of an individual.

In addition, the benefits of attending meditation retreats may be far-reaching, extending beyond just sleep benefits. Many people can attest to the fact that the mindfulness skills gained further help in decreasing anxiety, improving focus, and bringing a general sense of well-being. It is these more general benefits that, in turn, create a relaxed and balanced lifestyle, leading to good sleep hygiene.

In all, meditation retreats offer a potent opportunity for those seeking to reset their sleep patterns. By bringing together serene environments, structured practices, education, and community, retreats provide participants with the tools they need to transform their approach to sleep, making them a valuable option for those looking to profoundly improve their sleep health-and by extension, their overall quality of life.

Diet, Exercise, and Sleep Hygiene

Such a relationship is complex and one of deep influence; hence, it calls for mindful consumption in return by those desiring better rest. Food and beverages act not just as energy sources, but also as moderators of physiological processes, which include those related to sleep. It is the timing, composition, and quality of what we consume that can either nurture restful sleep or become a hurdle in the way of disrupting the natural sleep-wake cycle.

Foods have been in use for promoting the secretion of melatonin, an important hormone regulating sleep patterns. These include cherries, bananas, and oats that naturally contain or help the body synthesize this sleep-inducing compound. Those containing tryptophan, an amino acid that forms serotonin and melatonin, will promote good rest. Sources such as turkey, nuts, seeds, and eggs are great at dinner or over an evening snack when one desires to wind down. A healthy diet with such food gives the body building blocks it requires to transition easily into sleep.

On the other hand, heavy or rich meals, especially those with high fats or spices, can interfere with rest. Very often, when such food is taken near bedtime, it creates a lot of discomfort, indigestion, or even acid reflux, which could prevent the body from relaxing well. While sometimes comforting, late-night snacking has the potential for one unintended consequence: the activation of digestion during the time the body would naturally want to rest and repair.

On the other hand, sugar and refined carbohydrates can also disrupt this process when taken in excess. When this type of food raises blood sugar levels too quickly, the inevitable crash afterward can cause restlessness or wakings during the night. This causes an energy imbalance that negatively impacts progression smoothly through the stages of sleep, especially the restorative deep sleep that is needed to recover mentally and physically.

Among dietary elements affecting sleep, caffeine is probably the most known. Found in coffee, tea, chocolate, and energy drinks, it works as a stimulant by blocking adenosine, a neurotransmitter that induces sleepiness. Where an afternoon cup of coffee might be just what is needed to feel alert, consumption of caffeine during the late afternoon or evening can greatly delay sleep onset. Sensitivity to caffeine varies, but a general rule of thumb is to avoid caffeinated products at least six hours before bedtime to minimize their interference with rest.

Another important factor that should be considered regarding diet and sleep is alcohol. While it may initially act to relax someone and perhaps help them fall asleep more quickly, the overall effects are very negative. Alcohol interferes with the REM stage of sleep, thus fragmenting rest and impairing cognitive and emotional processing. This effect is amplified as consumption increases, and moderation is key for those looking to improve their sleep patterns.

Hydration plays a subtle yet important role in sleep quality. As much as the intake of water throughout the day helps the body maintain its functions efficiently, excessive fluid intake in the hours leading up to sleep causes one to wake up frequently to use the bathroom. A fine balance has to be struck between hydration and avoiding disruptions for uninterrupted rest.

Timing also plays a big role in how food and drink interact with sleep. Since the body's internal clock, or circadian rhythm, is inextricably linked to the digestion process, eating at consistent times throughout the day works agreeing that natural rhythm. Inversely, inconsistent eating times serve to disrupt it. This means dinner can be digested and out of the way by the time the evening naturally winds down.

The overall diet quality has far-reaching influences on sleep. Diets rich in whole, minimally processed foods provide vitamins and minerals that facilitate prime bodily function, which again includes sleep regulation. Magnesium is a mineral of relaxation that helps calm down; it is found in leafy greens, nuts, and whole grains. Deficiency in magnesium has been associated with insomnia and daytime throb in staying asleep. In this vein, vitamin B6, obtained from fish, poultry, and fortified cereals, is also involved in the synthesis of melatonin, again showing a relationship between a nutrient-adequate diet and improved sleep.

Processed and fast foods, full of unhealthy fats, excessive salt, and artificial additives, often lead to inflammation and other physiological imbalances that can affect sleep. Reduction in intake of such foods and focusing on nutrient-dense alternatives supports the body's ability to maintain energy levels during the day with steadiness and a restful state at night.

Herbal teas such as chamomile, valerian root, and passionflower have been used since time immemorial to induce sleep and, in a natural and mild way, prepare the body for rest. These teas contain compounds that induce relaxation and reduce stress, thus offering a soothing effect toward bedtime. They are a suitable alternative to caffeine-laden beverages in helping one get into a sleep-conducive ritual.

It also includes mindful eating habits, such as portion control, eating slowly, and savoring each bite. Overeating or gobbling down meals quickly can cause bloating or discomfort, which makes it difficult to fall asleep. The introduction of mindfulness in eating improves digestion and changes the relationship with food into a more harmonious and balanced one, which would ultimately lead to rest.

Understanding the interplay between diet and sleep equips individuals with the means to make conscious choices to improve their rest. This connection puts a strong emphasis on an integrated approach to wellness, wherein food serves not only as nourishment but also as a foundation for sound sleep. By paying attention to how certain foods and drinks affect the body, one can work agreeing the natural sleep-wake cycles to establish a diet that will help create a path toward better health and wellness. This attention to conscious eating establishes a strong link to further discuss other lifestyle elements, such as the contribution of exercise in the pursuit of rest, which even more strongly reinforces the journey toward refreshing sleep.

Exercise is a potent remedy for sleeplessness, and its benefits are not confined to physical health. Regular physical activity normalizes the body's circadian rhythms, which makes falling asleep and sleeping without interruptions much easier. The type of exercise, the timing, and even the intensity can all help or hinder its effectiveness towards sleep improvement, and activity selection is important to ensure a raise in heart rate yet also to be in conjunction with the body's desire for nighttime rest.

Aerobic exercise, otherwise popularly known as cardio, has been found to have immense effects on sleep quality. Running, swimming, cycling, and brisk walking all raise the heart rate and trigger the release of endorphins, chemicals in the brain that act as natural painkillers and mood elevators. These exercises can reduce the time it takes to fall asleep and increase the duration of deep sleep, the most restorative phase. However, there is an excellent time for aerobics; doing intense exercises within the same hours of going to bed can be very counterproductive since one's body will be too active for sleep. It is not advisable to try using such aerobic exercise as a way of inducing sleep, without excluding the unwanted rise in alertness, and therefore are usually best done three hours or more before bedtime.

Another positive factor in sleep is resistance training, or weight training and exercises that add resistance. This strengthening of muscles, alongside improving the general health of the body, helps alleviate some physical symptoms of stress and anxiety, both very common culprits of sleep disturbances. Such activities contribute to better sleep by promoting energy expenditure, hence helping to deepen sleep and reduce nighttime awakenings. Just like aerobic exercises, timing can often play a big role with strength training and its outcome with sleep. Generally, sessions that tend to help most at night are morning and early afternoon workouts, due to the increase in daytime energies in the body and the general fatigue at night, which most definitely will make the body get its rest.

Such light exercises as yoga and tai chi, which include certain elements of meditation and controlled breathing, work great for people who suffer from insomnia. Both practices are based on controlled movements and breathing, thus allowing a person to reach an emotionally and physically relaxed state that prepares the body for sleep. Different yoga styles allow one to practice everything from a vigorous sequence to more restorative poses, which might be done closer to bedtime to quiet the mind and transition the body into a state of readiness for sleep.

Besides these few specific types of exercises, regular walking included in the daily routine can be very helpful for sleep. Walking provides mild cardiovascular benefits and exposes the individual to natural sunlight, which helps the body regulate its internal clock. This is essential in maintaining regular sleep patterns and enhancing the quality of sleep.

Less intensive but equally important flexibility and balance exercises prevent falls and night injuries, especially among the elderly. Good balance and flexibility contribute to overall mobility and help reduce anxiety and stress from physical limitations that could be interfering with sleep.

For those researching the best types of exercises to help improve their sleep, it's important to consider the style of exercise, health status, and personal preference. A workout that is enjoyable and doesn't feel daunting will go a long way in being sustained for the long term. In fact, this consistency is what ensures full sleep benefits from exercise; physical activity proves most effective when it is regular.

It is also important to optimize the sleep-enhancing effects of exercise by embedding these physical activities into the broader practice of sleep hygiene. This would include going to bed and waking up at the same time every day, having a bedtime routine that signals to the body it's time to sleep, and creating an environment that is favorable for sleep. Details such as the right room temperature, minimal noise, and optimal lighting can significantly affect sleep quality and should be considered alongside exercise routines.

The ultimate result is that physical activity and sleep go in a circle. Inasmuch as regular physical activity may improve the quality and duration of sleep, a good rest itself may heighten the ability for physical performance and overall energy, which then again can make physical activity more feasible and enjoyable. Taking both sleep and exercise together, these can be mutually beneficial toward well-being and life balance.

Working in a complete pattern of sleep hygiene into your nighttime routine greatly enhances sleep quality, particularly when used in combination with meditation. These practices are supposed to create an ideal sleeping environment and pattern of behaviors that induce restful sleep. This technique will further enhance not only the effectiveness of meditation but also stabilize the circadian rhythms that help get deeper, more restorative sleep.

Establishing a routine sleep pattern is the first foundational basis of sleep hygiene. Consistency means going to bed and awakening at the same time day after day, including during weekends. This helps by consistently resetting your body's sleep-wake cycle to a certain timing, which can help people more naturally fall asleep and wake up. It's a good idea to get seven to nine hours of sleep at night, and then see how you feel during the day. If you are really struggling to make it through the afternoon and need two or three cups of coffee to get through it, you may need to increase the amount you sleep every night. Your sleep environment can greatly affect your sleep quality. Your bedroom should be designed as a sanctuary for sleep: controlling for light, noise, and temperature. A dark, quiet, cool environment helps signal to the body that it's time to wind down. Blackout curtains, eye masks, and white noise machines can all be very important tools. The ideal sleeping temperature is around 65 degrees Fahrenheit (ca. 18 °C). Different people, different strokes, the thing is to not make it too hot or too cold; that would be disruptive to sleep.

The hour of the night before going to bed is very critical to set up the scene for the night's sleep. A bedtime routine to calm down can make all the difference in falling asleep and in the quality of your sleep. This may be the reading of a book, taking a warm bath, or some light gymnastics or yoga. It is highly recommended to avoid stimulating activities like checking emails, intense exercise, or watching thrilling television shows. The blue light from screens on smartphones, computers, and televisions interferes with the production of melatonin, the hormone that tells your body it's time to sleep. Consider setting a "technology curfew" an hour before bedtime, and instead engage in activities that help your mind and body wind down.

Diet also plays an important role in sleep hygiene. What you eat and drink in the hours leading up to bedtime can have a major impact on how well you'll sleep. Heavy or rich foods can cause discomfort and indigestion, which may make it difficult to fall asleep. Furthermore, caffeine and nicotine taken in the late afternoon or evening will interfere with sleep since both substances stimulate the brain. Alcohol may make a person relax initially, but during the processing of alcohol, it can disrupt sleep during the middle of the night. These substances should be avoided during evening hours; if hungry, a snack high in protein is best before bed.

The effects of regular physical activity are that it may help you sleep more soundly and fall asleep faster. Timing is important, though: exercising too close to bedtime is stimulating. Workouts should be scheduled so that they are finished at least a few hours before going to bed.

You can incorporate mindfulness and relaxation techniques into your bedtime routine to help your mind get ready for sleep.

Activities like deep breathing, progressive muscle relaxation, or visualization of a quiet place can reduce anxiety and help relax the body. Regular meditation strengthens these benefits by training your mind to focus and redirect thoughts that often lead to insomnia.

Finally, pay close attention to your sleep pattern and the sleep environment. A sleep diary is a good record of bedtime, wakening time, and feelings during the day. After some time, patterns may become obvious that help you realize which sleep hygiene practices are effective for you. Modify the practices as necessary, based on your findings, for ever-improving quality of sleep.

Building proper, balanced sleep hygiene practices will lead to an environment that fosters not just sleep itself, but also effective meditation. The interplay between organized sleep hygiene and meditation may just enhance overall well-being in your life, building a better foundation toward optimized mental and physical health.

Measuring Progress and Adjusting Practices

Every program that seeks to enhance sleep and meditate requires you to be able to understand your progress and make needed adjustments in practice. This way, you are on your way to reaching set goals and personalizing the approach such that, when need be, it easily changes with the needs that you will have. Monitoring and adjusting form part of perfecting the sleeping and meditation techniques with a view to fine-tuning your routine accordingly for maximum effect.

Start by setting specific, measurable goals related to sleep and meditation habits. This could be a necessity of increasing your average sleeping from six to eight hours daily, or the less time taken to fall asleep. In meditation, it may be a target aimed at increasing the time duration of the session or generally the quality of the states of relaxation during the sessions. Having these targets provides for a clear point against which you can measure progress.

Monitoring one's sleep can be done at various levels, from basic to sophisticated. One of the more simple ways involves a sleep diary. In this way, you're able to track times and patterns and note any improvements you might be making. In the morning, write down what time you went to bed and woke up, how long it took to go to sleep, how often you woke up, and the quality of the sleep. Over time, this journal will reveal patterns and triggers that affect your sleep quality, such as dietary habits, stress levels, and environmental factors.

The nature of wearable devices-automatically tracking sleep duration and quality, stages-can even be done by wearable watches or fitness trackers. These often give very insightful reports on sleep architecture, detailing how much REM, light, and deep sleep you get every night. More enlightening, the information obtained from such a perspective will reveal physiological aspects of one's sleep that would, otherwise, not be obvious in mere introspection.

Apart from the mechanical tracking, consider subjective measures of your sleep quality. Every day, note how you feel when you wake up and during the day: rested and energized, or tired and sluggish? In this way, you can correlate the quantitative data with your real physical and mental state and get a holistic view of your sleep health.

While a little more subjective, meditation progress also can be followed well. Keep a meditation log in which you note the length of sessions, techniques tried, and your subjective experiences during and after each session. Were you able to focus or was your mind wandering? Were you more relaxed or agitated after sitting? Over time, these entries will provide you with information about the most effective techniques for you and the best times of the day.

Apps specifically designed for meditation can help track progress. Most of those timed apps provide feedback on numerous days per period and total time in your practice. They can have guided sessions that help your practice become more regular. They will also give some idea of how your practice develops over time.

As you start gathering data on your sleep and meditation, the next step would be to analyze this information to make informed adjustments. If your tracker shows that you are consistently not reaching the recommended stages of deep or REM sleep, consider modifying your pre-sleep routine or bedroom environment. Maybe you need to limit exposure to blue light from screens earlier in the evening, adjust the temperature of your bedroom, or change your mattress or pillow.

Similarly, if in your meditation logs you recognize that some techniques work much better for you in your relaxation or focusing, favor these in your routine. If you find that it gets you more prepared to face the day, compared to evening meditation, in which you are less successful, adjust your schedule.

Your goals should periodically be reconsidered to check if their outcomes are what you intended because your needs and situation continue to evolve. By this time, you shall advance further and may note spots to pay more focused attention on dream recall and learn how to meditate elsewhere. All these on-track monitoring and adjusting not only achieve better sleep and immediate results of meditation but build onto long-term wellness and resiliency.

The path of sleeping better and meditating more effectively is deeply personal and constantly evolving. In continuously charting your progress, being prepared for change allows you to develop a practice that is dynamic in its potential to create great enhancement in the quality of life, keeping both sleep and meditation sharp as tools for personal growth and health.

As you get up and running on your meditation journey to better sleep, you may find that your needs evolve as your sleep does. This is quite normal, and part of the process reflects the dynamic nature of personal health and wellness. It is adapting these techniques to align with these changes that will be important for sustaining the gains you make, and pushing forward into new levels of health and awareness. It provides great adaptability, both immediately, enhancing the quality of sleep, and for long-term sustainability.

You might, at the beginning, focus on certain strategies in your meditation practice that work for the most problematic part of your sleep pattern, such as not being able to fall asleep or to stay asleep. As these issues become regulated or resolved, the emphasis of meditation could shift. It's wonderful to recognize these shifts and adjust your approach accordingly to meet the changing needs of your body.

One of the important points about adjusting your meditation practice, as your sleep improves, relates to the length and type of meditation you do: perhaps shorter sessions were sufficient, or maybe you needed only those types of meditation aimed at relaxation and stress relief. This could be in extending sessions or trying new styles, as one finds more depth in tranquility or control regarding sleep. In other words, it may come with progress from a first basic mindfulness exercise to yogic sleep and guided visualizations by benefiting from elements that are new to him now that his ability for relaxation has improved.

Moreover, the timing of your meditation can also make all the difference. While meditation before bed initially helped quiet your mind for sleep, you may find that doing this earlier in the evening-or even in the morning-leads to greater calm that can serve you throughout the day and thus indirectly helps you sleep better. This can help decrease reliance on meditation to sleep and encourage a more integrated approach to mindfulness in your life.

The content of your meditation sessions can also evolve. Initially, focusing solely on relaxation and the physical sensations of breathing could have been effective. As you grow in your practice, incorporating elements that address cognitive and emotional processing-such as gratitude meditation or cognitive defusion techniques-can help in managing the thoughts and worries that often precede sleep disturbances. Such evolution in content deepens your practice and expands the range of benefits that you experience, contributing to both better sleep and improved mental health.

Another important adjustment is related to technology and tools: Initially, the guidance of apps and sessions can be very helpful; the more advanced you are in meditation, the better and more effective unguided sessions might feel because through self-direction and your inner feeling for meditation, even deeper benefits can be released. This progression can develop a stronger sense of autonomy and personal link in your meditation practice, further enhancing the benefits.

It is, however, important to monitor one's progress to understand when and how such adjustments must be made.

Ongoing assessment of how one feels through the day, energy levels, mood, and quality of sleep can yield very useful feedback regarding the effectiveness of current practices and may indicate when changes could be beneficial. Tools like sleep trackers or meditation apps that provide detailed feedback on your sessions can be very instrumental in this evaluation process.

As your mastery of meditation deepens, so does your need to be abreast of the latest research and developments in sleep science as well as meditation practice. The study of new research, books, or workshops refreshes your practice and may even introduce you to new techniques or refinements that will further improve the quality of your sleep.

Lastly, know when to get professional help. If, with improvements, new or returning sleep challenges start to affect your life considerably, then this is the right time to consult a health professional or a specialist in sleep disorders, since they may be able to offer you some personalized stratagems for overcoming certain specific sleep disorders that could underlie. Your journey into better sleep must be effective and informed if you are to get the best options toward sustaining and improving well-being.

Meditation is a powerful tool to improve sleep and overall well-being, but occasionally, it may not be enough to deal with serious or persistent sleep-related issues. Knowing when to seek professional help may make all the difference in your health and ensure you get the most appropriate and effective treatment. This section will take you through how to recognize signs that indicate the need for professional intervention and what one may expect from such intervention.

However, in many instances, stubborn sleep disorders, such as chronic insomnia, sleep apnea, and restless legs' syndrome, may require somewhat more than meditation and good sleep hygiene. If you have been meditating for quite a while and do not experience any improvement in sleeping, or if it has gotten worse, this may now be a good time to decide to get professional help. These specialists are specially schooled in sleep medicine, and so they may deal with the diagnosis and treatment only fitted for your condition.

It's essential to monitor the frequency and severity of your sleep disturbances. Occasional sleepless nights might not be cause for concern, but consistent patterns of poor sleep can lead to long-term health issues, including cardiovascular disease, diabetes, and depression. If you find yourself waking up frequently throughout the night, struggling to fall asleep almost every night for weeks, or feeling excessively sleepy during the day, these are strong indicators that you should consider professional guidance.

Another red flag is when one's sleep problem starts encroaching on one's daytime life. Sleep deprivation negatively impacts one's ability to think, including cognitive impairment in memory, judgment, and decision-making ability, and affects one's emotional well-being by showing signs of irritability and mood swings; this further puts one at an increased risk of mental disorders. If you find that your work performance is suffering, relationships are suffering, or you're relying heavily on caffeine or other stimulants to get through the day, these are signs that sleep problems are taking a considerable toll on your quality of life.

Finally, if your sleeping problem is followed by high blood pressure, weighing, and/or weakening immunity, do not hesitate but look for your healthcare provider; these all might be symptomatic of sleeping disorders such as sleep apnea that a meditation habit, alone without medical support, will just not get better. Start with Your Primary Care Provider. They can provide you with a preliminary diagnosis of your sleep disorder and refer you to a specialist in sleep disorders if necessary. Be prepared to discuss the details of your sleeping habits, meditation practices, and other health issues. It would be helpful to keep a sleep diary for a couple of weeks before your appointment, noting the times you go to bed and wake up, how often you wake during the night, and how you feel in the mornings.

A sleep specialist may recommend that one undergo a sleep study, also called polysomnography, to diagnose the sleep disorder correctly. This study can be conducted in most instances at a sleep laboratory overnight and may monitor brain waves, oxygen level, heart rate, breathing, as well as eye and leg movements. The results will help the specialist whether you have a sleep disorder such as sleep apnea, periodic limb movement disorder, or narcolepsy and, based on the diagnosis, development of a treatment plan for you.

Treatment of sleep disorders is often based on the diagnosis, but it usually involves a combination of medication, therapy, and changes in lifestyle. If you are diagnosed with sleep apnea, you may be prescribed a CPAP machine to help keep your airways open while you sleep. In cases of insomnia, they may recommend cognitive-behavioral therapy for insomnia, also known as CBT-I; this type of therapy can help change thoughts and behaviors that make sleep difficult.

In addition to medical treatments, a healthcare provider can offer guidance on how to integrate meditation more effectively into your treatment plan. They can help tailor your meditation practices to address specific symptoms or issues, enhancing the benefits of your existing practice.

It is also important to know the signs that will show your condition is improving or if there is something that needs to be adjusted in your treatment plan. Regular follow-ups with your healthcare provider will ensure your approach remains effective and is adjusted to your progress.

Knowing when to seek professional help and acting on it is very crucial in managing severe sleep problems effectively. While meditation brings numerous benefits, it's also important to know when more specialized medical intervention will be required, either for the underlying conditions or even for more complex sleep disorders. Seeking professional help at the right time will ensure that you are taking the most comprehensive approach toward improving your sleep and safeguarding your health.

The Future of Sleep and Meditation

The swiftly developing area of research has drawn neuroscientists and clinicians into the spotlight regarding meditation and sleep as they strive to find new ways toward the quality of life with improved rest and psychological well-being. With meditation becoming more forceful in the field of medicine and general health, the integration into the area of sleep science means the beginning of a very promising frontier that is constantly unwinding. It covers the latest findings in deep exploratory reasoning in the way they open doors to new applications and interventions for improving sleep with the help of meditation.

Interest from the scientific world in how meditation impacts sleep has been increasing rapidly for numerous years due to the increase in sleeping-related disorders across the globe. Meditation, previously primarily intended for stress reduction, has become an increasingly investigated activity in scientific research regarding cures for various sleep problems, including insomnia and disordered sleep. In so doing, most studies conducted often indicate that these practices influence brain patterns and are thus likely to directly impinge on mechanisms of sleep regulation.

Perhaps one of the most critical aspects of this research is related to the influence of mindfulness meditation on sleep architecture-the structure of different stages that every individual goes through every night. According to these studies, mindfulness practices significantly enhance the density of rapid eye movement sleep, highly responsible for emotional regulation and memory retention. This again becomes pivotal because disruptions of REM sleep are related to a host of psychological afflictions, including higher stress levels and depression.

Additionally, there is the interaction of meditation with the circadian rhythm, which is the internal body clock that dictates the sleep-wake cycle. Preliminary findings indicate that regular meditation may help synchronize this internal clock with the natural environment, promoting more consistent sleep schedules and thus alleviating symptoms of sleep disorders such as delayed sleep phase syndrome.

Another exciting development of this area is the examination of meditation's role in enhancing sleep quality among older adults, who become particularly vulnerable to sleep disruptions with physiological changes accompanying aging. Indeed, mindfulness meditation has been shown to improve sleep quality in older individuals by way of reducing sleep onset latency and decreasing nighttime awakenings, thereby countering the age-related decline in sleep quality.

These changing studies are being reinforced, little by little, from neuroimaging and physiological data. For example, fMRI brain scans have shown that meditation involves the activation of areas responsible for regulating sleep in the brain, including the prefrontal cortex and anterior cingulate cortex. Besides, neurophysiological studies have begun to clarify how meditation influences the activity of the autonomic nervous system, which suggests that it enhances parasympathetic responses-the part of the nervous system responsible for 'rest and digest' functions-which may in turn promote better sleep.

Still being developed, like any ongoing research, what it is learning and continuing to build further develops meditation techniques for better integration into everyday life. Various applications and wearable devices include special meditation modes intended to favor sleep quality and duration with monitoring by patterns. This will go a long way in facilitating meditation at ease, but also tracking how meditation styles may affect an individual's ability to fall asleep.

The future will further ensure even more advanced integrations of biotechnology and machine learning into meditation practices for sleep optimization. Advancements in wearable technology are foreseen to deliver even more precise measurements of physiological changes during meditation and sleep, thus offering customized suggestions for improving sleep based on individual data.

As this segment of health technology develops, it most definitely will be associated with interventions that are increasingly personalized, adaptable to the unique biological and psychological profiles of any given individual. This would not only enhance the effectiveness in using meditation as an intervention for sleep improvement but would also widen its scope of applicability across demographics and needs.

The direction taken by research in the areas of sleep and meditation, in fact, points in the direction of an inclusive health care approach where preventive steps and natural therapies take an equal place with pharmaceutical interventions. The move is indicative not only of a broader shift in conceptualizing and treating sleep disorders but also in increasing awareness of the interdependence among mind, body, and well-being.

Standing at the threshold of new discoveries in the field of sleep science and meditation, the potential to improve lives across the world only grows. This chapter lays a foundation for such an understanding, setting the stage for consideration of how technology might even further revolutionize our approach to achieving restorative sleep through meditation.

This increasing innovation has brought into the health and wellness environment a new world of tools for improving personal health and, most recently, much emphasis on enhancing sleep with meditation practices. This is evident from the strong trend in developing and spreading apps and devices aimed at aiding meditation with a view to better sleep-a convergence of technology with traditional techniques. These tools democratize access to meditation practices, adding layers of convenience and effectiveness to make the practice easier to engage in and sustain over time.

Today, a wide array of mobile applications are available that cater to the needs of individuals looking to enhance their sleep through meditation. These guided meditation sequences, bedtime stories, breathing exercises, and ambient sounds are all combined to help the user fall asleep and remain in a very docile state throughout the night. What really sets these apps apart, however, is how personalized the experience can be for the user. User responses are fed into algorithms that then adapt the content to serve an individual's needs for relaxation and sleep, hence making the meditations more effective. This goes beyond software to wearable devices that record sleep patterns and physiological reactions during meditation and rest. These wearables come either as wristbands or fitted into bedding accessories and provide real-time heart rate, respiratory rate, body movements, and even REM cycles. This data is important in understanding sleep architecture and any disturbance that might occur. More importantly, these devices can then provide feedback and suggestions on the data collected, like the best times to sleep and wake up, hence optimizing sleeping.

Further utility of such devices is introduced by their integration with smart home technology. For example, wearable sleep trackers, communicating with home automation systems, can modulate lighting, temperature, and sound levels in the bedroom to create an ideal environment for relaxation and sleep. Such smooth integration helps in creating a sleep-conducive environment and makes the process quite effortless for the user, hence encouraging habituation.

These technological solutions are, in equal measure, supported by growing research evidence that shows how they improve sleep quality. There is evidence that meditation application users may record significant advancement in sleep duration and quality, reduced time to fall asleep, and reduced reliance on sleep medications. Similarly, people who have started using sleep trackers tend to be more aware of their sleep and follow regular sleep patterns, which are very important for maintaining health and wellness.

Moreover, these technologies keep on improving. The newest wave of apps and devices use artificial intelligence and machine learning to be more predictive and give finer-grained advice. For example, some apps include voice recognition that picks up on stress or anxiety in the user's voice and recommend meditations to address those issues before they become overwhelming.

Despite impressive capabilities, these technological aids are not without their limitations. Issues have arisen over data privacy and interpretation of health data. It also presents the risk of over-reliance on technology for sleep at the expense of direct engagement in meditation practices. These challenges, however, are recognized both by developers and health professionals who work together to address them, ensuring that these tools are secure and complementary and not a replacement for the traditional practices of meditation.

As we look to the future, technology in sleep and meditation will only continue to evolve. Future generations of innovations will include advanced biosensors that detect and analyze even more complex physiological signals, virtual reality environments that better simulate soothing natural settings, and AI-driven coaching that personalizes and adapts in real time to a user's emotional and physical state.

These technologies are not only a new frontier in the improvement of sleep and personal health, but they also form a different paradigm in our understanding of and interaction with our bodies and minds. In that sense, for those people seeking to improve their sleep through meditation, they present an enormous promise by making such practices more accessible, enjoyable, and effective. The journey towards better sleep and well-being is ongoing, with these technological aids guiding us down this path in an important way.

The work of working your way toward sleep with meditation is a bit like learning a new language: it takes patience, practice, and a commitment to continual growth and understanding. Once the basic mechanics of meditation have been learned and one has begun to get the deep and profound effects it can have on sleep and overall well-being, there is an understandable curiosity as to what lies beyond. The road does not stop at simply overcoming sleepless nights or at the capability of not getting distracted during meditation. This, therefore, opens the gateway for the deeper exploration and integration of such practices into your day-to-day life.

What that means will be different at different times for each person and will change with the person, needs, and desires. Most likely, you will notice over time that your meditation will become more than just a way to sleep better, but a source of great insight and peace that affects the way you interact with the world.

One of the first things that might be considered part of your continuing journey involves deepening your meditation practice by either lengthening the duration of the sessions, experimenting with various meditation styles, or using more advanced techniques targeted at areas like compassion, loving-kindness, and advanced visualization. Such practices will help further in improving the quality of sleep and strengthening one's emotional resilience, providing a greater sense of balance, and reducing tension in daily life.

Another important way of developing your practice is to keep a reflective journal. Writing down what has happened can be very useful as it may help you see patterns and note development and changes in your mind, emotions, and body. This will also help you in ongoing decisions as to where in your practice you feel you are working most effectively, and what you need to change or perhaps explore.

Education is also key to deepening your understanding and sustaining your practice. Reading the latest research on meditation and sleep, attending workshops, and participating in seminars can offer new insights and techniques that help deepen your practice. This can keep your practice fresh and continually evolving.

You may also want to share your knowledge and experiences with others as a rewarding next step in learning to manage your sleep through meditation. Teaching meditation to people or leading small groups not only deepens one's practice but also allows others to learn the benefits of meditation for sleep. This is most effective in communities where sleep disorders are rampant, and the habit of meditation is not practiced.

Other important steps would involve integrating meditation more fully into your life. This can be through creating spaces around your house that promote peace and tranquility, to incorporating mindfulness into your day, other than just for the times when you really meditate. This one can easily bring mindfulness with you while you eat, walk, or even right at work, and with this, you'll make it through your day very calmly and focused.

As already discussed, technology can also support your practice to move forward: guided meditation apps or those that help you track your progress will reinforce your daily practices and give valuable feedback. A number of these applications have communities with which you can connect, sharing your experiences and learning from others.

A longer-term growth of other avenues may be inspired by exploring the role of meditation in a wider health context. It is well documented how meditation influences stress, anxiety, and physical health, like blood pressure and immune response. Gaining an understanding of these connections can serve to further motivate you in your practice and encourage its continued growth as part of a holistic approach to health.

Lastly, be open to your practice adjusting with the change in life. Flexibility in adjusting meditation techniques according to the current situations and needs is an important factor that will help in sustaining one's practice. This can include adjusting your schedule, new forms of meditation, or simply adjusting your focus-each of these adjustments responsive to your life situation helps ensure that your meditation practice will continue to grow and enhance your life.

In a nutshell, the journey through meditation to better sleep is only the beginning. Deeper self-awareness, health, and fulfillment will follow in lifelong exploration. As you continue to explore and integrate meditation into your life, remember that each step forward offers a chance to discover more about yourself and the profound impact mindfulness can have on your well-being.

Conclusion

The reflective approach shows that the content of this book has taken us deep into a tour of how meditation can affect sleep quality and, overall, our health. The journey through the pages have equipped us not just with theoretical knowledge but also with practical tools to reshape our nightly practices and, in turn, our lives. This synthesis aims at putting together what we have learned and the importance of changing our lives by incorporating meditation into our sleep habits.

From the very first discussions on the nature of sleep and the debilitating effects of insomnia, we dove deep into the scientific underpinning that links meditation to enhanced sleep quality. We show the stages of sleep and how disturbances in these cycles can lead to a host of health issues, emphasizing the necessity for approaches that foster deep and restorative rest. Meditation hence emerged in this scenario as an important solution that could provide the bridge to better sleep, without necessarily having to use pharmaceutical interventions.

We have explored different types of meditation-any one of which may be more suitable for various tastes and purposes. Among those discussed were mindfulness meditation, centered on the present moment, which encourages a non-judgmental awareness, and focused attention practices, helping to stabilize the mind and ward off the scattering impact of stress and anxiety. Techniques such as body scans and guided visualizations were discussed in terms of their ability to directly address the physical and mental obstacles that can prevent a peaceful night's sleep.

This was very practical advice, further extended into the physical realm, where ways of cultivating a sleep-conducive environment were discussed. External factors such as light, sound, and temperature can favorably align with the internal clock of our body and go a long way in improving the quality of rest. The role of diet and exercise also came into their own in offering a holistic approach to sleep hygiene, complementing the mental and emotional benefits derived from meditation.

From this, the narrative takes the reader forward to emphasize the consistency and persistence of practice. The deeper effects of meditation, in sleep in particular, are to be gained when the practice is regular and a part of daily routine. There is a flexibility in meditation techniques, and it grows with the practitioner to give deeper and more profound benefits. This adaptability means that as the needs and circumstances of practitioners continue to change, their practice evolves, which means their growth is continuous.

We also discussed the future and some emerging research that has been continually validating and building on our understanding of meditation's role in health and well-being. The integration of technology in this field, through apps and devices, provides exciting opportunities to enhance our practice and gain deeper insights into the physiological and psychological aspects of meditation.

Continuing to develop into this, the encouragement for you is to remain interested in and proactive in exploring these depths of meditation. Remember, the practice is dynamic, not static; and in continuous exploration and adaptation, that will keep it alive. Every new research, evolving technique, and personal insight will take constant shape and redefine the experience. It is a dynamic process that has kept meditation so up to date, with strong potentials to support sleep, besides other problems of living and to really make an effect in many areas of life for betterment. Meditation teaches that the journey of improved sleep through meditation itself is enlightened; it goes beyond restorative rest-actually, a beginning to enhanced self-realization, better emotional stability, and more positive physical health. Every step on this journey equips you with the power to combat the ups and downs in life with strength and poise. With each page that you flip, with every practice that you apply into your life, remember, meditation is all about learning, practicing, and growing in that circle. This is no ordinary book; it is a guide on your way to a better, healthy, and harmonious lifestyle.

As we come to the end of this exploration into meditation and sleep, let's not forget that learning and growth are lifelong processes. The journey you have undertaken in bringing meditation into your life is one that invites ongoing discovery and evolution. Opening to this path involves commitment not only to practice, but also to ongoing inquiry and openness to new knowledge. This section is reserved for reinforcing the importance of continuing with your meditation to expand and deepen your practice continually.

Meditation, like any other skill, benefits a great deal from regular practice. The changes it can bring about in your sleep patterns and overall well-being can be profound, but they are most often realized through persistent and dedicated practice. It is easy to get discouraged if the results are not immediate or if there are setbacks along the way. Yet, the very nature of meditation is based upon patience and persistence. Each session builds upon the last, and over time, the cumulative effects can be transforming. The encouragement here is not just to stick with a routine, but to stay curious and open to evolving your practices. As you grow, as life changes, your needs and interests in meditation may change, too. What works for you today may need adjustment tomorrow. This is, in fact, one of the strongest points about meditation: whether it is new stressors you are trying to handle, changing health conditions, or simply deeper relaxation and rest, meditation gives you an adaptive toolkit.

Exploration to deepening in meditation practice could also include trying new techniques, joining a community of practitioners, reading new research about the subject, and possibly attending workshops or retreats. Each of these activities can provide fresh insights and inspire you to integrate new elements into your practice.

Furthermore, exploration means bringing the principles of mindfulness and meditation into various areas of your life. Consider how these principles might affect your eating, physical activity, relationships, and work. Meditation is much more than a method to sleep better; it is a way to be more mindful, present, and joyful in life. Benefits start to show their ripples in every nook and cranny of your life when the practice is extended beyond the cushion or mat.

The engagement in a community is also of immense importance while building up or deepening your practice. It would be helpful and motivating for a person to either join or set up a meditation group. The communities hold a certain treasure of knowledge and experiences brought together, which helps at times of difficulties by raising the bar, offering connectivity that enriches the practice.

Keep in mind that the way of meditation is different for everyone. It is somewhat of a personal journey-a journey to which external support may be beneficial but is internally driven. Your meditation growth and how it aids your sleep and overall health are very personal and will happen in due time. Trust the process, and don't be too hard on yourself in the process. Patience and persistence are your friends in this regard.

In cultivating this practice that is ongoing, consider keeping a meditation journal. Writing down your experiences can help you to notice subtle changes that may be easy to miss on a day-to-day basis. Over time, these entries will build up as encouraging proof of benefits and growth you are experiencing. They may also serve as a reflective tool for yourself, helping you to understand more clearly your mental patterns and triggers, which is so important for personal development.

As we come to the closing remarks of this book, remember that meditation is a practice, but also much more-it is a life choice with many great rewards and one that takes a commitment and a curiosity to explore. The journey does not end here; it evolves and expands as you do. What you have learned throughout this book serves as an introduction-the basic building blocks to get you ready to keep exploring, learning, and growing with meditation.

Embracing meditation as a lifelong companion for better sleep and improvement in overall well-being is not an addition of habit but the relationship transformation of self to one's mind, body, and the very concept of rest. A journey, deeply profound, which continuously keeps on evolving once one starts the trip of implementation of meditation in life. But with all due respect, it doesn't require commitment, per se; rather, in the most important sense, it allows one to draw closer to oneself and be more in tune with life.

Meditation by nature is a form of practice in awareness. That is, observing the mind without attachment, recognition of bodily sensation without judgment, and regulation of emotions so as neither to suppress nor overindulge them. You begin naturally to extend this awareness to sleeping, too, making sure you do the things that will let you get restful nights. More aware of what your body wants and what goes through your mind, you began to notice all the things, even minute ones, which affect your sleep patterns.

Probably the most important insight meditation provides is realizing that sleep is not a passive condition but an active process of restoration, so important for our physical health and psychological well-being. In this respect, through meditation, one learns to smoothly pass into sleep and thus not to spend so much time in bed without sleeping. Meditation teaches you to let go of the cares of the day and lapse into a state of relaxation that promotes easier sleep onset and better quality of sleep.

Furthermore, meditation arms you with ways to cope better with the stressors in daily life. Stress is one of the major disruptors of sleep, and by managing your stress through meditation, you are tackling one of the key causes of insomnia directly. This not only serves to help one sleep more soundly, but also fosters resilience that equips one to meet life's ups and downs with much more equanimity.

Embracing meditation as a lifelong practice is to accept it in both the easy and sleepless nights. The continuity of practice is what is essential, not just when there are sleeping problems but as a preventive measure. This consistency reinforces the benefits of meditation, potentially making each successive night's sleep more restorative.

With time and with more practice, you'll also notice that the beneficial results of meditation accumulate. The layers of wellness impregnate everything from your sleep to your life's details. A person practicing meditation regularly may show greater concentration, lesser anxiety, increased emotional stability, and a deeper layer of happiness. Such improvement will surely help one stay more active in life with much satisfaction, which also allows for automatic quality sleep.

Going forward, meditation to sleep more effectively is not about overcoming insomnia or any form of sleep disorder, but an important lifelong skill to enhance your general quality of life. This involves reflecting on progress from time to time, openness to adjusting one's techniques, and the willingness to go deeper with time as your experience and confidence increase. This journey also invites the spirit of exploration: the exploration of various meditation styles, perhaps inclusions of mindfulness techniques, or guided visualizations, and even integrations of other supportive practices such as yoga or tai chi. Each of these can complement your meditation practice and enrich your sleep hygiene for an integrated approach to wellness.

Thereby, as with meditation, sleep improvement takes a path of people going together on a course. Community and connection also benefit greatly by being taken into this area. To get community engagement, therefore, deepens such support in more insight and offers different perspectives than can enhance the practice tenfold. Share your findings or learn from others-whether an online forum, local group in meditation, or simply among friends-sharing increases the positivity and will probably encourage times that can be very frustrating.

As we close this exploration, remember that the true essence of embracing meditation for better sleep is in the small daily steps you take. Every moment of mindfulness, every evening of preparation for rest, and every night of restorative sleep builds on the last. Meditation is not just a solution to sleep problems but a gateway to a more attuned and fulfilled life. It promises not only a better sleep but a more enriched, aware existence. May the practices and principles you have learned continue to take you deeper into rest, better health, and greater peace as you keep moving forward on this journey.

Thank you very much for choosing this book.

I hope you found it enlightening and beneficial in your pursuit of better sleep and wellness through meditation.

Your feedback is invaluable to me and to others who might be considering this book. If you enjoyed your journey or found the practices helpful, please consider leaving a review.

Your insights not only assist potential readers in making informed decisions but also support me in growing and improving as an author.

Thank you once again for your support and happy meditating!

Evelyn Foster

www.ingramcontent.com/pod-product-compliance
Lightning Source LLC
Chambersburg PA
CBHW072335270726
48659CB00022B/1603